Donald J. Trump Posts From His Truth Social ✅
@TrumpDailyPosts

HAPPY EASTER TO ALL, INCLUDING CROOKED AND CORRUPT
PROSECUTORS AND JUDGES THAT ARE DOING EVERYTHING POSSIBLE
TO INTERFERE WITH THE PRESIDENTIAL ELECTION OF 2024, AND PUT
ME IN PRISON, INCLUDING THOSE MANY PEOPLE THAT I COMPLETELY
& TOTALLY DESPISE BECAUSE THEY WANT TO DESTROY AMERICA, A
NOW FAILING NATION, LIKE "DERANGED" JACK SMITH, WHO IS EVIL
AND "SICK," MRS. FANI "FAUNI" WADE, WHO SAID SHE HARDLY KNEW
THE "SPECIAL" PROSECUTOR, ONLY TO FIND THAT HE SPENT YEARS
"LOVING" HER, LONG BEFORE THE GEORGIA PERSECUTION OF
PRESIDENT TRUMP BEGAN (AND THEREBY MAKING THE CASE
AGAINST ME NULL, VOID, AND ILLEGAL!), AND LAZY ON VIOLENT
CRIME ALVIN BRAGG WHO, WITH CROOKED JOE'S DOJ THUGS,
UNFAIRLY WORKING IN THE D.A.'s OFFICE, ILLEGALLY INDICTED ME ON
A CASE HE NEVER WANTED TO BRING AND VIRTUALLY ALL LEGAL
SCHOLARS SAY IS A CASE THAT SHOULD NOT BE BROUGHT, IS
BREAKING THE LAW IN DOING SO (POMERANTZ!), WAS TURNED DOWN
BY ALL OTHER LAW ENFORCEMENT AUTHORITIES, AND IS NOT A
CRIME. HAPPY EASTER EVERYONE!

Donald Trump Truth Social 01:21 PM EST 3/31/24

ROUGH BEAST

Who Donald Trump Really Is, What He'll Do if Re-Elected, and Why Democracy Must Prevail

*An Urgent Appeal to Independents, Undecideds,
Fiscal Republicans, Third Party People,
Voters Who "Don't Like Politics,"
and the Biden-Hating Left*

GREG OLEAR

Paperback ISBN: 979-8-218-43519-6
Ebook ISBN: 979-8-9859319-4-5

Turning and turning in the widening gyre
The falcon cannot hear the falconer;
Things fall apart; the centre cannot hold;
Mere anarchy is loosed upon the world,
The blood-dimmed tide is loosed, and everywhere
The ceremony of innocence is drowned;
The best lack all conviction, while the worst
Are full of passionate intensity.

Surely some revelation is at hand;
Surely the Second Coming is at hand.
The Second Coming! Hardly are those words out
When a vast image out of Spiritus Mundi
Troubles my sight: somewhere in sands of the desert
A shape with lion body and the head of a man,
A gaze blank and pitiless as the sun,
Is moving its slow thighs, while all about it
Reel shadows of the indignant desert birds.
The darkness drops again; but now I know
That twenty centuries of stony sleep
Were vexed to nightmare by a rocking cradle,
And what rough beast, its hour come round at last,
Slouches towards Bethlehem to be born?

—William Butler Yeats, "The Second Coming"

For my father

INTRODUCTION
Slouching Towards Dictatorship

DONALD TRUMP'S TERM IN OFFICE can be summed up in four words: *pandemic, protest, impeachment*, and *insurrection*. He left the White House with 392,428 Americans dead of a plague he exacerbated; with Washington recovering from a coup attempt he instigated; with the economy teetering towards recession; with our standing around the world at its lowest point in a century; and with the U.S. an additional $8 trillion in debt.[1] He had, by far, the lowest average presidential approval rating since Gallop started keeping track in 1938, and was widely reviled abroad. Four of the five largest protests in the history of the country happened on his watch. He was impeached twice. He could have been impeached a third time, in 2019, after the release of the Mueller Report—which, contrary to what Trump

---

[1]   The debt stood at $27.68 trillion, to be exact, up from just under $20 trillion when Trump took office.

and the mendacious Bill Barr told us, did *not* exonerate him. Even his much-ballyhooed campaign promises fell flat: He failed to build the wall, and he failed to drain the swamp. He did, however, watch a lot of television and play a lot of golf.

In the various presidential surveys taken since Donald left office, historians have consistently ranked Trump dead last, behind even the contemptible white supremacist Andrew Johnson and the hapless James Buchanan. This is not recency bias. By any metric, Trump was a catastrophic failure: corrupt, sociopathic, cruel, venal, disruptive, artless, dumb, and pathologically inept—a terrible president and an even worse human being. He threw paper towels at hurricane victims! He called veterans of our armed forces "suckers and losers!" He invited the Taliban to Camp David! He banked $2.4 billion in emoluments during his four years in office! He characterized the neo-Nazis at Charlottesville as "very fine people!" He nominated an(other) alleged sexual assailant to the Supreme Court! He sat on his ass watching TV as his besiegers stormed the Capitol! He humped a flag! And that's just off the top of my head.

We have never had a monster like this in the White House. No one comes close. That the country managed to survive four years of Trump suggests that Otto von Bismark was on to something when he remarked that God seems to have a special providence for the United States of America. With Donald, we dodged a big orange bullet.

In a word, we were *spared*.

And yet as I write this, Donald John Trump is the presumptive nominee of one of our two major political parties. Only two individuals have a legitimate chance at winning the White House in November—I'll talk about the myth of third parties and the perils of voting for the nihilistic likes of Robert F. Kennedy, Jr. in Chapter 9—and Trump is one of them. And he's not *just* that political party's nominee. Donald Trump has subverted the entire GOP, purged it of the disloyal, and taken total command. He installed his daughter-in-law—Lara Trump, desecrator of Tom Petty's memory and wife of Eric Trump (Donald's son who ripped off his own cancer charity)— as co-chair at the RNC, and changed the organization's rules there so that the lion's share of donations will be used to cover his mounting legal bills. As I explore further in Chapter 8, the conventional, old-school Republicans of yesteryear have either retired, lost, died, or kissed the ring. Don't be fooled by the cute elephant logo. Whatever the branding, this is no longer the Party of Lincoln. There is no GOP anymore, only MAGA. It is an entire party built around a demagogue with dictatorial ambitions.

If the polls are to believed, that demagogue has a coin flip's chance of retaking the White House. Like, *this might actually happen*! People in my family are going to vote for him. People in your family are probably going to vote for him, too. And if, God forbid, he succeeds, there are—as I explain in Chapter 7—a rabid battalion of religious zealots, Christian nationalists, and reactionary monarchists poised to make so many drastic changes to the country so quickly that the United States won't be recognizable by the Fourth of July 2025. The threat is real. The situation is dire.

This isn't me, a known "TRUMP HATER," trying to frame the narrative to make Donald look bad. All of what I'm saying here is objectively true, as this book will make abundantly clear. As the kids say: #Facts.

To which you might ask: Says who? Who is this Greg Olear guy to make such grandiose claims? Since 2017,

I've been writing, researching, reporting, podcasting, broadcasting, and tweeting about Trump. In my regular column and on my interview podcast, PREVAIL, I cover politics, history, national security, foreign affairs, organized crime, dirty money, global corruption, and the fight for democracy. I've written extensively about Trump, Vladimir Putin, Jared Kushner, Rudy Giuliani, Leonard Leo, Brett Kavanaugh, and other characters in the MAGA universe. The PREVAIL archive—some of which was appropriated to produce this book—is vast. When I started covering Trump in 2017, I could be dismissed as a mere novelist. Not anymore. This has been my job for over seven years now.

In May of 2018, I published a short book called *Dirty Rubles: An Introduction to Trump/Russia*. In the introduction, I wrote: "Donald Trump is nothing less than a threat to the American way of life. His term in office comprises an existential threat to the republic, the gravest since the Civil War. Not since 1860 has the future of the *Union itself* been in such doubt. Other presidents might have lacked good judgment, but we never questioned where their true loyalties lay. George W. Bush loved America, Richard Nixon loved America, Herbert Hoover and Warren G. Harding loved America. Trump loves only himself, cares only about himself, is loyal only to himself. And Vladimir Putin has exploited this weakness, to the detriment of not just every American, but every freedom-loving human being on earth."

All this was true six years ago—before the four indictments and the fraud case and the defamation lawsuit; before his Russian strongman idol invaded Ukraine; before the Big Lie and the insurrection; before the two impeachments; before the covid response he horribly mismanaged; before Volume 5[2] and the Mueller Report; before the Brett Kavanaugh confirmation hearing—and it's doubly true now. The stakes have never been higher.

A second Trump administration would bring about the end of American democracy, full stop.

Academics who study authoritarian movements, scholars of fascism, foreign correspondents and government employees who work in other countries and know first-hand what corrupt autocracies look like—I've interviewed quite a few of these experts on my podcast over the last three years—are in consensus on this.

The United States is slouching towards dictatorship. Party of Lincoln, you say? If Trump wins, the fallen at Gettysburg will have died in vain; a government of the people, by the people, and for the people *will* perish from the earth.

Maybe you disagree. Maybe you think I'm full of crap, or have some ulterior motive, or am on George Soros's payroll. Maybe you have a soft spot for Donald Trump, or find him amusing, or loved him on *The Apprentice*. Maybe you like that he says the quiet part out loud, because you share his feelings about immigrants. Maybe you think he's the victim of a Deep State conspiracy, a witch hunt, a Russia hoax. Maybe you believe there is no discernible difference between Democrats and Republicans, or Donald Trump and Joe Biden. Maybe the *Dobbs* ruling that overturned *Roe v. Wade* doesn't concern you. Maybe you are reluctant to vote for Joe Biden because of his age, or his support

---

[2]   Full title: *Report of the [Bipartisan] Select Committee On Intelligence, United States Senate, On Russian Active Measures, Campaigns and Interference in the 2016 U.S. Election, Volume 5: Counterintelligence Threats and Vulnerabilities*

of Israel, or his choice of vice president, or his alleged financial enrichment by some Ukrainian company his son sat on the board of a decade ago. Maybe you find James Comer and Jim Jordan credible. Maybe you dismiss me—and the fascism scholars, and the foreign correspondents, and the government workers, and the experts in authoritarianism—as a flock of Chicken Littles. Maybe you're sure that we're all being dramatic. Maybe you think, like those good Germans in the last days of the Weimar Republic, that what Trump plans to do couldn't possibly happen *here*.

If so, my friend, this book is for you.

That is my purpose: to show you who the real Donald Trump is (a lifelong criminal); to remind you of Trump's unprecedented failures as president (almost four hundred thousand dead of covid on his negligent watch, two impeachments, and an insurrection); to explain what he's planning to do if he wins (install himself as dictator, dismantle the federal government, criminalize abortion in all 50 states, impose an autocratic system that will strip away rights from most Americans); and to impress upon you the ugly future we have to look forward to if the Rough Beast prevails—especially if we're trans, gay, Black, brown, a Trump-critical journalist, an immigrant, a migrant, a refugee, a rape victim, from another country, from a Democratic-leaning voting district, poor, working class, or a woman. On the pages that follow, I make this urgent argument. I also want these pages to serve as a time capsule, so that future generations—assuming they survive the ravages of climate change Donald's policies would accelerate—will know what it was like, living in the United States of America a quarter of the way through the 21st century.

Am I getting all worked up over nothing? Do I suffer from Trump Derangement Syndrome, as the social media trolls contend? Is this just a ploy to convince you to vote for an unpopular incumbent? Donald Trump can't really be *this* bad, can he?

Read on and decide for yourself.

I

DISHONEST ABE
Lies, Damned Lies, and Stuff Donald Says

The Argument: Trump is a serial liar.

THE TRUMP PRESIDENCY began with an assault on the truth.

The first time that Sean Spicer, the newly-minted press secretary, addressed the White House press corps, he lied about the size of the crowd at the Inauguration—and he did so at the new president's stubborn insistence. Spicer may as well have been standing next to Shaquille O'Neal, indignantly insisting *he* was taller. We knew he was lying, *he* knew he was lying, the press corps knew he was lying, *Saturday Night Live* certainly knew he was lying.[3] Even Chuck Todd, no journalistic paragon, took exception to it, in what turned out to be an historic episode of *Meet the Press*, on which Trump advisor Kellyanne Conway coined the term "alternative facts." There was uneasiness, certainly, and plenty of jokes made at Spicer's expense. But few imagined that this pathetic spectacle was merely the opening salvo in a four-year onslaught against reality.

Trump's war on the truth did not begin when he took office, of course. Maybe it started when Jeff Zucker, president of CNN, gave him all that free airtime and presented him, falsely, as a serious presidential candidate. Maybe it started when *The Apprentice* showrunner Mark Burnett packaged him, falsely, as a successful, self-made billionaire, trust-washing him for the American public. Maybe it started when Trump joined Twitter, and opted to insert the word "real" in his handle, before his actual name. Or maybe it started on his first visit to Moscow in 1987, when the KGB began cultivating him in earnest (of which more in Chapter 2). Whatever the case, the annihilation of truth is Trump's greatest achievement as president—his lone success. During those miserable four years, reality was not the winner.

So many lies! So much gaslighting! So much B.S.!

The first chapter of *Dirty Rubles* is called "The Russia Lie." I wrote,

> Throughout the campaign, during the transition period, and after inauguration, Donald Trump and his surrogates vehemently denied meeting with Russians of any stripe, for any purpose. Every time they were asked about a connection between

---

[3]   SNL's decision to cast Melissa McCarthy as Sean Spicer helped seal his doom as press secretary.

the campaign and the Kremlin, they shot it down. And they were *indignant* about it. The response was always something along the lines of, "Russia? Us? How dare you accuse us of such a thing!"

and then listed *17 separate times* Trump or one of his proxies flat-out lied about his connections to the Kremlin. These were, I pointed out,

all lies—the same big lie, repeated over and over. This repetition of the "Big Lie," it should be noted, is a propaganda technique developed by the Nazis. Hitler wrote about it in *Mein Kompf*, one of very few books Trump is believed to have read. Either way, Trump has employed the Big Lie technique for years—lying regularly about his wealth (he lied his way onto the *Forbes* wealthiest Americans list), his fitness (he coerced his physician to lie about how healthy he was), his sexual prowess (a tabloid headline allegedly from ex-wife Marla Maples, saying Trump was the best sex she'd ever had), and so forth.

But this was different. This wasn't about the size of his bank account, his good cholesterol levels, or his penis. This was about national security, about cozying up to an enemy. And yet still, Trump and his minions went on TV, took to Twitter, stood behind the podium in the White House Press Room, and lied egregiously to the American people, over and over and over and over.

I wrote that in 2018. The lies kept on coming. The lies *still* keep on coming. With Donald Trump, the lies never stop.

We were told that Trump's campaign was self-funded; it wasn't. We were told that he would drain the swamp; he didn't even try. We were told that he would bring his successful businessman's experience to Washington; this is a man who went broke *running a casino*. We were told Jared and Ivanka would be a moderating influence; they may well be more ghoulish than Donald. We were told Trump would release his taxes; the alleged audit outlasted his presidency. We were told he would release Melania's immigration paperwork; we're still waiting. We were told a wall would be built, and we were told Mexico would pay for it; a wall was not built, and Mexico did not turn over a single peso. We were promised a better healthcare plan than Obamacare; the ready-in-two-weeks details are yet to be revealed.

We were told Trump was the healthiest president of all time ever; he isn't. We were told he was 6' 3" / 239; he's well shorter than that, and far heftier. We were told the midnight run to Walter Reed in November 2020 was the first part of a physical, a cover story even the press seemed to realize was bunk in the moment; we still don't know why he was rushed there. (Panic attack? Stents? Exorcism?)[4] Even when white powder flew out of his nose on live TV, even when he appeared impaired, his eyes dilated, not a single member of the media told us about his drug use—despite Noel Casler, a talent handler on *Celebrity Apprentice* and an eyewitness, repeatedly insisting, including in an interview with me, that Trump was an habitual user.[5]

---

[4]   The latest word is that Trump went for a routine colonoscopy.

[5]   A Pentagon IG report on pharmaceutical mismanagement in FPOTUS's White House Medical Unit confirmed the use of drugs in the Trump White House: "We concluded that all phases of the White House Medical Unit's pharmacy operations had severe and systemic problems due to the unit's

We were told there was no communication between Russia and anyone associated with Trump or his campaign; turns out, Donald Trump, Jr., Jared Kushner, Paul Manafort, Roger Stone, Michael Cohen, Jeff Sessions, Mike Flynn, Carter Page, and George Papadopoulos, at a minimum, all communicated with Putin's proxies. We were told the Mueller investigation was a witch hunt; it was actually a hunt for traitors, and it found plenty. We were told Trump would be tough on Putin; he capitulated to him like a sniveling BDSM bottom in the world's least sexy bondage club.

We were told the novel coronavirus was like the flu. We were told it was a hoax. We were told it was under control. We were told it would be gone by Easter, 2020. We were told that one day, it would just go away, like a miracle. We were told the Democratic governors were to blame. We were told Fauci was not to be trusted. We were told the CDC was not to be trusted; instead, we should put our faith in Michael Caputo, a GOP dirty trickster who once worked for Vladimir Putin, and whom Trump inexplicably installed as a spokesman at Health & Human Services. We were told Mike Pence, who as governor of Indiana presided over the worst U.S. HIV outbreak in the last 20 years, was the best man to manage the pandemic response. We were told that he did a fantastic job. We were told masks didn't work, that wearing them was government overreach, an assault on

---

reliance on ineffective internal controls to ensure compliance with pharmacy safety standards...We found that the White House Medical Unit provided a wide range of health care and pharmaceutical services to ineligible White House staff in violation of Federal law and regulation and DoD policy. Additionally, the White House Medical Unit dispensed prescription medications, including controlled substances, to ineligible White House staff."

our freedoms. We were told it was safe to reopen months before it was. We were told herd immunity was a smart strategy. We were told that certain already-available drugs treated covid-19 just fine. We were told the infection rate would be lower if we did less testing. We were told the virus wasn't especially contagious, even as it spread like wildfire through the West Wing. We were told the effects were not that bad, even as Chris Christie spent a week in the ICU, even as Herman Cain died. We were told the Trump Administration's handling of the pandemic was top notch, despite Jared Kushner killing a plan devised by his own hand-picked advisors that would have saved countless lives, especially in Blue States. We were told that the pandemic was over, even as the death toll hit 350,000. We were told that upon taking office, Joe Biden would immediately shut down the country because he was a pawn of China who would use the virus as an excuse to establish a Communist government in Washington.

We were told there would be a pivot.

We were told Trump was strong. We were told Trump was a fighter. We were told, on those rare occasions when he read from the teleprompter without going off script, that he was "presidential." We were told he cared about people. We were told he cared about the victims of the hurricane in Puerto Rico. We were told he isn't a sexist, isn't a racist. We were told he was only joking.

And then there were all the lies about the 2020 election, and the fake electors, and the voting machines, and Trump's failed coup attempt of January 6, 2021—lies that are now immortalized in a House investigation report and scores of criminal trials.

"Who are you gonna believe," Chico Marx famously quipped, "me, or your lyin' eyes?"

And now? Cleft by seven years of pounding by a psychological battering ram—four years with Trump in the White House, three with him out—our national reality is fractured. Alternative facts prevail. There is no universal, agreed-upon truth. And this is exactly what we were warned during the Reagan years that the Russians were trying to do to us, via psychological warfare: "Change the perception of reality of every American to such an extent that, despite the abundance of information," explained KGB defector Yuri Bezmenov back in 1984, "no one is able to come to sensible conclusions."

Mission accomplished, comrades.

But wait—what would Donald Trump know about the KGB?

II

MAFIA DONALD
You Can't Spell "Trump" Without "RU"

*The Argument: Trump is a lifelong criminal
and a longtime Kremlin asset.*

IN THE EARLY 90s, a New York executive who worked for a prominent financial services company flew to London to attend a conference. While there, he hobnobbed with another executive, an American who worked in the firm's Moscow office. Accompanying the Moscow executive were some Russian nationals—KGB officers moonlighting as security and logistics detail for the company.

And that is how the New York executive came to have dinner with a small group of Soviet spies. When the topic turned to the Big Apple, he was surprised to hear that the KGB officers were very familiar with Donald Trump. Trump was a fixture in the New York tabloids, and had been for years, but at the time, he was hardly world famous. The reason the KGB officers knew about Trump, the executive soon realized, is because Trump was being cultivated by that organization. This was such an open secret in Soviet intelligence circles that Russian spies were boasting about it 30 years ago at a restaurant with a total stranger.

This colorful anecdote was related to me by the New York executive, who is now retired. By itself, it's just that—a colorful anecdote. "Hey, remember the time we went to dinner with the KGB guys?" Taken together with many similar data points, however, it establishes a narrative—that Donald Trump *really was* cultivated by the Russian intelligence services. That he really was—really *is*—a Kremlin asset.

There is plenty of reporting to support this:

Trump first got on the KGB's radar in 1977, when he married his first wife, Ivana Zelníčková, a Czechoslovakian national who, against all odds, managed to emigrate from that closed Eastern Bloc country to Canada. The investigative journalist Luke Harding writes about this in his book *Collusion: Secret Meetings, Dirty Money, and How Russia Helped Donald Trump Win* (2017): "According to files in Prague, declassified in 2016, Czech spies kept a close eye on the couple in Manhattan....There was periodic surveillance of the Trump family in the United States. And when Ivana and Donald Trump, Jr., visited [her father] in the Czechoslovak Socialist Republic, further spying, or 'cover,'" he writes. "Like with other Eastern Bloc agencies, the Czechs would have shared their intelligence product with their counterparts in Moscow, the KGB."

Investigative journalist Craig Unger's book *American Kompromat: How the KGB Cultivated Donald Trump, and Related Tales of Sex, Greed, Power, and Treachery* reveals that Trump's first known direct encounter with the KGB took place in 1980, when he purchased television sets for his new hotel project at a Russian-owned electronics store, Joy-Lud—"an important outpost for the KGB," Unger writes, "Crazy Eddie with a Russian accent, always filled with KGB agents and high-level Soviet dignitaries."[6]

One of Unger's sources for *American Kompromat* was the ex-KGB officer Yuri Shvets, a Soviet defector, who in the 1980s worked in counterintelligence for the KGB in Washington. While he was not personally involved with the recruitment and handling of Trump, Shvets knew well the spy agency's M.O. The KGB employed "spotters," he explains in *American Kompromat*, who were on the lookout for possible American assets. In a media interview with Unger to promote the book, Shvets said he believed that the KGB began cultivating Trump in 1983, three years after initially identifying him as a possible asset.

But it wasn't just Russian spies Trump was mixed up with. It was also Russian mobsters.

"MONEY LAUNDERING" is a benign-sounding euphemism for "making the revenue collected from drugs, sex

---

[6]   Both of the owners of that long-defunct store—Semyon "Sam" Kislin and Tamir Sapir—would pop up later in the Trump chronicles. The former was a big donor to Rudy Giuliani's various campaigns; the latter helped finance the Trump Soho project.

trafficking, arms dealing, diamond smuggling, extortion, and other malefic activities seem like it was earned by legitimate means, so it can be spent with impunity." It was pioneered by the visionary gangster Meyer Lansky in the thirties and forties, and perfected by the Kyiv-born mafioso Semion Mogilevich, the presumptive head of the Solntsevskaya Bratva, the premier Russian crime syndicate, in the eighties and nineties.[7]

Any ambitious goon can work a protection racket, run numbers, deal drugs, traffic prostitutes, or do professional hits. It requires only muscle, will, an appetite for risk, and a sick disregard for human life. The big-time money launderer, on the contrary, must be bright enough to understand how to work the books, creative enough to seek out new avenues and opportunities, and ruthless enough to apply these skills to something not only criminal, but heinous. Such individuals are rare. As Craig Unger explains in *House of Trump, House of Putin,* "it was Mogilevich's expertise at laundering money that made him so invaluable to other mobsters. He had mastered a skill that was deeply coveted by the most formidable gangsters on the planet: He took dirty money and made it clean." The so-called "Brainy Don" was able to both stockpile *and* launder the money, making him very powerful indeed. And very, very rich.[8]

---

[7]   For more on the birth of organized crime and the intersection of mobsters and spies, check out my friend Stephanie Koff's episodic podcast "The World Beneath." She and it are my main source for understanding the Russian mob.

[8]   At Citjourno, Stephanie Koff, aka Lincoln's Bible, and Louise Neu outline the relationship between Mogilevich and Vladimir Putin in "Poke the Bear," published in November of 2017. There is even a video of the two of them together the night of Putin's election.

The money launderer might not be the one who cuts the heroin with lethal amounts of fentanyl, or rapes the fifteen-year-old sex slave trafficked from El Salvador, or sells the enriched uranium to Al Qaeda. But by abetting these abominable activities with his financial chicanery, he is complicit in those crimes. None of this bothered the heartless Mogilevich, who got his start as a simple con man, ripping off his fellow Soviet Jews who were leaving the USSR for Israel or the West.

In the mid-eighties, Donald Trump began to sell condos to individuals with close ties to Russian organized crime. In 1984, the Soviet soldier-turned-mobster David Bogatin, a close associate of Mogilevich, plunked down $6 million in cash for five of Trump's condos. Per David Cay Johnston in *The Making of Donald Trump*, Trump Tower was one of just two buildings in all of New York City that allowed units to be purchased by anonymous shell companies. Any subsequent revenue generated from that transaction—maybe there was rental income, maybe the units were sold—was "clean."[9] This was hardly the only shady real estate deal Trump was involved with.

As Anders Åslund, the Swedish economist, put it to Craig Unger: "Early on, Trump came to the conclusion that it is better to do business with crooks than with honest people. Crooks have two big advantages. First, they're prepared to pay more money than honest people. And second, they will always lose if you sue them because they are known to be crooks."

---

[9]   In Bogatin's case, the apartments weren't the savviest investment. The government seized all five units after he pleaded guilty in a gasoline bootlegging scheme involving Mogilevich in 1987, explaining that he used the real estate to "launder money, to shelter and hide assets."

For Trump, the beauty part was that, when he sold those units to the Russians, he wasn't technically breaking any laws. He was getting all of the reward while taking none of the risk—other than the inherent risk of doing business with mobsters.

In 1986, at a luncheon given by the cosmetics magnate and philanthropist Leonard Lauder, Trump met Natalia Dubinina, the daughter of the Soviet ambassador to the United States, Yuri Dubinin. After flattering him by complimenting Trump Tower, she invited him to visit Moscow. The following year, he took her up on the offer.

"On July 4, 1987,"—the Fourth of July—"Trump flew to Moscow for the first time, together with Ivana and Lisa Calandra, Ivana's Italian-American assistant," Harding writes in *Collusion*. "Moscow was, Trump wrote, 'an extraordinary experience.' The Trumps stayed in Lenin's suite at the National Hotel, at the bottom of Tverskaya Street, near Red Square…. The hotel was linked to the glass-and-concrete Intourist complex next door and was—in effect—under KGB control. The Lenin suite would have been bugged."

These encounters are all corroborated by newspaper reporting, as well as by Unger, in *American Kompromat*.[10]

Upon his return from that fateful 1987 Moscow trip, Trump began to branch out in his interests. "For the first time he gave serious indications that he was considering a career in politics," Harding points out. "Not

---

[10]   Yuri Shvets theorizes that Trump's handler at the time may have been Natalia Dubinina's then-husband Alexander Yakovenko, who was then posted to the U.N. Yakovenko later served as the Russian ambassador to the United Kingdom from 2011-19, a period of increased Russian espionage activity in Great Britain.

as mayor or governor or senator. Trump was thinking about running for president."

In 1988, Trump flirted with the idea of entering the presidential race, going so far as to deliver a speech in New Hampshire. He toyed with running again in 2000, on the Reform Party ticket, even hiring his old chum Roger Stone to run an exploratory committee before ultimately dropping out.

The Russians never seriously believed the buffoonish Trump could ever win the White House. Yuri Shvets quipped, "If you had told anyone at the KGB [back then] that Donald Trump would one day be president, they would not even laugh, because it was too ridiculous."

The nineties were unkind to Donald John Trump. The Bush I recession hit his businesses hard. Early in the decade, Trump filed for bankruptcy protection for Trump Taj Mahal (1991) and Trump Plaza (1992). In between those bankruptcy filings, he lobbied Congress for tax relief for real estate developers, began phoning reporters claiming to be a publicist named John Barron, had an affair with a D-list actress named Marla Maples, and divorced his wife of 14 years, the mother of his kids Donald, Ivanka, and Eric: the by-then-also-famous Ivana Trump.

Moscow had also fallen on hard times. The Soviet Union collapsed on Christmas Day 1991. What the West viewed as the triumph of capitalism over Communism was really the subversion of a conventional superpower by the shadowy forces of transnational organized crime. The Cold War was not over; it just shifted modes of attack. In the early nineties, Russia invaded the United States—not with soldiers, but with mobsters.

The commander of this underworld incursion was a violent ex-con named Vyacheslav Ivankov, known as "Yaponchik," or "Little Japanese." Hardened in the brutal

Soviet prison system, Ivankov was a *vor v zakone*, or thief-in-law—the brand of criminal that originated in the post-Second World War gulags. He was such a nasty, violent S.O.B. that when it was necessary to rough someone up to extort them, he didn't send in a subordinate—he did the job himself. This was the guy the Solntsevskaya Bratva posted to Queens, which was both the command center for the Russian mob in the Northeast U.S. and the hub of Fred Trump's real estate empire.

Ivankov arrived in the U.S. in 1992, ostensibly to work in the film industry. The new Russian government warned the FBI that he was up to no good. But the feds lost track of him almost immediately, even as he traveled from New York to Florida and everywhere in between, consolidating power. Per the testimony of Bob Levinson,[11] then the FBI's foremost Russian mob expert:

> Ivankov's organization's income was derived from a number of sources: his group was implicated by sources to have been involved in the "gasoline tax scam" whereby so-called "daisy-chains" of petroleum handling companies were established with the specific intention of defrauding governmental tax authorities using non-existent or ghost companies to pay the gasoline taxes due.

> A primary source of the group's funds was the collection of "krisha" or protection money from wealthy Russian and Eurasian businessmen operating between North America and the former Soviet

---

[11]   Levinson disappeared in 2007 on Kish Island, Iran, while working a mission for the CIA. He was believed to be held by Tehran. In 2020, his family announced that he was presumed dead.

republics. In addition, the Ivankov organization organized the collection of, in effect, a "street tax" from Russian-born and Eastern European criminals who were operating their illegal enterprises in North America. Ivankov organization members fanned out across the United States and Canada identifying and then approaching these criminals saying that each now had to contribute to an "obshak" (mutual benefit fund) being collected and organized by the Ivankov group.

In addition, Ivankov and other members of his organization settled business disputes for Russian and Eastern European businessmen operating between North America and the former Soviet Union, receiving in return a percentage of the amount in dispute, usually hundreds of thousands of dollars. Through his authority as a "thief-in-law" and the head of a criminal organization, Ivankov was able to exercise a kind of informal power in the émigré business community tantamount to decisions made by formal, official courts of law. Those who went against the decisions made by Ivankov and his associates were usually met with violence, including beatings and/or murder.

As Little Japanese worked the States, Semion Mogilevich set up his base of operations in Budapest. In 1991, he married Katalin Papp, a Hungarian national, and through that marriage was able to acquire a Hungarian passport—making it easier for him to travel.[12] He soon

---

[12]   Levinson, the FBI agent, moved to Budapest around this time, to investigate Mogilevich more closely.

acquired a bank in Russia, which allowed him access to the global financial system.

For three fruitful years, Ivankov did his thing, laying the foundation for what would become the world's pre-eminent organized crime operation—more *S.P.E.C.T.R.E.* than *GoodFellas*. He ran amok. Law enforcement had no idea where he was....until, one day in 1995, they found him living in a deluxe apartment at—you're not gonna believe it—Trump Tower. And that was not the only Trump property he frequented: Ivankov was also a regular at the Trump Taj Mahal in Atlantic City. He was arrested in June of 1995, convicted, imprisoned, and deported to Russia in 2004 to face murder changes. Once home, he was promptly acquitted. He was gunned down in Moscow in 2009.[13]

This heinous monster was living in Trump's building, gambling in Trump's casino!

What was Donald Trump doing in 1995, when Ivankov got busted? Failing tremendously. That was the year when he declared a loss of an unfathomable $916 million on his tax returns. It was also at this time that Trump Tower became a sort of Moscow on Fifth Avenue, with any number of Russian mobsters scooping up apartments. As the ex-KGB officer Yuri Shvets put it, "The whole Trump Organization was turned into a money laundering front for the Russian intelligence community."

To anyone familiar with the real Donald Trump, this did not come as a surprise. Gangland was his milieu. He was, after all, a creature of the criminal underworld: a rough beast.

---

[13]   Why yes, it IS weird that Ivanka's name is so similar to Ivankov's. Thanks for asking!

In the early 1980s it was decided—by whom, and for what ultimate purpose, we can't say for sure—that Donald Trump would build a casino complex in Atlantic City, New Jersey—probably the most mobbed-up municipality in the Garden State. Dealing with the mafia might have dissuaded some developers from pursuing a Boardwalk Empire, but not Trump. He was uniquely suited to forge ahead.

Donald's father, the Queens real estate developer Fred Trump, had worked closely with Genovese-associated and -owned construction entities since building the Shorehaven development in 1947, when Donald was still in diapers (the first time around). Fred was an early mob adopter, the underworld equivalent of an investor who bought shares of Coca-Cola stock in 1919. The timelines are important to remember here. Organized crime did not exist in any meaningful way in the United States until Prohibition. Born in 1905, Fred Trump was just two years younger than Meyer Lansky. Thus, Donald Trump is *second generation* mobbed-up.

When Donald first ventured from Queens to the pizzazzier borough of Manhattan in the seventies, he entered into a joint business deal with "Big" Paul Castellano, head of the Gambino syndicate, and Anthony "Fat Tony" Salerno, of the Genovese family he knew well through his father and their mutual lawyer Roy Cohn.[14] As part

---

[14]　As Stephanie Koff, aka Lincoln's Bible, creator of "The World Beneath" podcast about mobsters and spies, told me in 2020: "To best understand Fred, just track his rise from single-family home construction to big residential developments. From Shore Haven (1947) to Beach Haven to Trump Village, all were done with known mafia partners, in Genovese-controlled territory, and eventually with a fully Genovese-owned construction company (HRH Construction). When the Russian mafiya began rolling in, they landed in Fred's properties and partnered

of this arrangement, Trump agreed to buy concrete from a company operated jointly by the two families—and pay a hefty premium for the privilege. Only then, with double mob approval, could he move forward with the Trump Tower and Trump Plaza projects.[15]

Atlantic City is in South Jersey, closer to Philadelphia than New York, so to build "his" casino, Trump needed to play ball with the Philly mob. That meant dealing with Nicodemo "Little Nicky" Scarfo, head of the most powerful mob family in Philadelphia. Land that Trump needed for his casino was owned by Salvie Testa and Frank Narducci, Jr.—hit men for Scarfo, collectively known around town as the Young Executioners (the nickname was not ironic). To help negotiate the deal, Trump hired Patrick McGahn, a Philly-based attorney known to have truck with the Scarfo family.[16]

---

with the Genovese on some big ticket scams. This was also during the time that Fred and his attorney Roy Cohn set up S&A concrete (via Nick Auletta)—a joint venture between Tony Salerno (Genovese boss) and Paul Castellano (Gambino boss), so that [D]onald could build in Manhattan. Remember [D]onald's quote, "Even my father, he said, you don't want to go to Manhattan. That's not our territory."? That's because Manhattan, for construction, was Gambino territory. They controlled the concrete and unions. And Fred was a very loyal, shrewd front for the Genovese. To get his idiot, greedy kid into Manhattan, Fred and Roy Cohn had to get those two mob bosses to agree on a joint venture."

[15]   Among Cohn's other clients at the time was Rupert Murdoch, whom he introduced to Trump in the seventies; you would be hard pressed to find three more atrocious human beings.

[16]   The last name should sound familiar; Don McGahn, the former White House Counsel, is Patrick McGahn's nephew. And Don McGahn is not the only Trump Administration hire with ties to the Philly mob. Among Little Nicky's associates was one Jimmy "The Brute" DiNatale, whose daughter, Denise Fitzpatrick, is the mother of none other than Kellyanne Conway. A number

Trump acquired the needed Atlantic City property at *twice* the market value: $1.1 million for a lot that sold for $195k five years before. But there were legal pratfalls, shady dealings, chicanery with the documents. The New Jersey Gaming Commission was investigating the matter, because casino owners could not, by law, associate with criminals. And most of Trump's friends were crooks. It looked like Trump was in trouble—not only of losing his gaming license, but of criminal indictment.

And then, something miraculous happened. On November 4, 1986, Scarfo and eleven of his associates were indicted on charges that included loan sharking, extortion, and conducting an illegal gambling business in a racketeering conspiracy. Prosecutors had tried for years to take down Little Nicky. And now, after all that time, they finally had their evidence. Not only that, but the investigation into Trump? It went away. Poof—as if it never existed.

Neat trick!

Protected by his father, by Roy Cohn, by the heads of the various crime families, and by friendly agents at the FBI (more on that in a minute), Trump was so untouchable that even the notorious mob boss Sammy "The Bull" Gravano couldn't get to him. On his podcast, Gravano recounts dealing with The Donald back in the day:

> It's very hard to fuck with Trump. His jobs are hundreds of million-dollar high rise construction,

---

of wiseguys paid their respects at DiNatale's 1983 funeral. I don't want to make the mistake of condemning Conway or Don McGahn for the sins of their relations. But given Trump's organized crime background, it's fair to question why he chose two children of mobbed-up families for his inner White House circle.

and they are all union. He has around him ex-FBI
agents as security. He came from a wealthy family.
He was not self-made. His father was a heavy-
weight construction guy with a ton of money and
a ton of connections: with the government, politicians, the FBI. When you start getting people that
connected, fucking with them is not a smart move.
Trying to shake them down is not a smart move.

Trump may not have been *self*-made, but he was sure
as hell made.

IF DONALD TRUMP IS A CROOK, why was he never
indicted until after he left office?

Occam's Razor says to reject the premise: the lack
of rap sheet means he's not a criminal. But in this case,
William of Ockham's principle of parsimony does
not hold. Trump is *absolutely* a criminal. He tried to
overthrow the government. He used the office of the
presidency to enrich his personal fortune. He obstructed
justice like it was going out of style. He directed his
personal attorney to violate campaign finance law by
paying off a porn star. He laundered money for individuals with ties to the Russian mafia. He benefited
from a real estate maintenance fraud scheme devised
by his father, Fred (who was himself involved with a
crime syndicate). He is a serial sexual predator. He
raped a well-known journalist in a department store.
He sexually harassed women on the set of his reality
show. He sent goons to steal his medical records and
menace his doctor. He skirted regulations prohibiting
cavorting with crime figures when running his casino.
He misrepresented his net worth and his income on loan
forms. He dodged the draft through bogus disability

claims. He socked his teacher when he was in grade school. And that's just the stuff we know about.

So, yes, he's a crook.

Why was he never charged with a crime during his real estate career?

It is inconceivable that a mobbed-up developer—a shady character to whom the government of Australia would not grant a gaming license because of his obvious mob connections; the subject of a 41-page initial investigation by the Department of Gaming Enforcement in the State of New Jersey that, taken together, is positively damning—could have avoided indictment for all these years *unless* he was covertly helping out law enforcement, as a Confidential Informant. Secret immunity would certainly explain why the FBI has given Trump a wide berth.[17]

But there are other, more human, motives at work as well, as the investigative journalist and author Craig Unger told me when I interviewed him on my podcast. Why, he wonders, didn't the FBI pay more attention to all the criminality surrounding Trump, especially during his run for president? Why did they turn a blind eye?

"And I say this knowing that they *had* to know this," he says, "because a lot of my material came from FBI files! So they certainly knew about it," *it* being Trump's dalliances with the Russian mob. Unger suggests that it was the culture of the Bureau, and the New York field office specifically, that made agents think twice about going down the Trump-Russia rabbit hole, telling me:

---

[17]   It is Stephanie Koff who first made the argument that Trump is a C.I. She has been calling for the intelligence community to release its files on him since 2016.

What American lawyer wound up representing Semion Mogilevich? It was of course William Sessions, who had been Director of the FBI. And you had people like James Kallstrom, who was a very high-ranking FBI official in New York, who was very close to Donald Trump . . . . Think about that. Let's assume you were a career FBI guy, and you've been there 20 years, and you're in the New York office. How vigorously are you going to pursue someone like Donald Trump? How vigorously are you going to pursue the Russian mafiya when your former boss is [Mogilevich's] lawyer? . . . And Donald Trump has given your immediate bureau director, James Kallstrom of the New York office—has given $1.3 million to his favorite charity. And several other FBI officials, when they retire, they end up doing security for Donald Trump, getting cozy jobs maybe making a couple hundred thousand dollars a year while they're still collecting their FBI pensions. Are you really going to put everything on the line to go after these guys?

In *American Kompromat,* Unger describes the afore-mentioned relationship between Trump and the FBI's James Kallstrom, whose unlikely friendship began in 1973. The former was pretty clearly cultivating the latter; since when does Trump give $1.3 million to *anyone,* and not expect something in return? Since when does he give that much money to *charity?* His M.O. is to promise but not deliver. As Unger diplomatically put it in his book, "Their relationship was such that Kallstrom said things about Trump that were diametrically opposed to the way most Americans saw him."

During their decades-long friendship, Unger writes, Kallstrom rose to a position of prominence at the Bureau: assistant director in charge of the New York field office, the FBI's largest—and the one right in Trump's backyard. He worked closely with Rudy Giuliani on the Mafia Commission Trial. And while he retired in 1997, he remained an influential figure in New York law enforcement until his death in July of 2021. Would Trump have continued to cultivate the friendship if Kallstrom wound up leaving the FBI in the eighties to work in, say, property management? Would agents in the New York field office have handled differently the Anthony Weiner laptop brouhaha that ultimately cost Hillary Clinton the election, if their old boss had not been such a vocal supporter of Donald Trump? If Kallstrom had not done interviews claiming that HRC was a criminal?

NPR interviewed Kallstrom in 2016, a week before the election, in the wake of the Comey letter. He said, "I don't say this politically; I just say this is a matter of law. The Democrats nominated someone to run for president that had a long trail of things that could be considered by a grand jury as being criminal." But he *was* being political. He allowed his personal bias—the wool Trump spent 40 years pulling over his eyes—to override his professional objectivity. Maybe it was too painful to admit that his good buddy was nothing more than a front for organized crime. That he'd been played.

Here I should stress this point: The Bureau is not a monolith. There are plenty of exemplary FBI agents. I'd venture to guess that *most* FBI are excellent. It was the excellent ones who Trump went after in the media when he was president: Andrew McCabe, Bruce Ohr, Lisa Page, Pete Strzok, and the former director, Robert Mueller.

Unfortunately, the *leadership* of the FBI has been suspect for most of its history. In a top-down organization, the personality of the guy in charge carries enormous weight. The opportunistic egomaniac J. Edgar Hoover ran the Bureau for almost 37 full years until his death in 1972. William Sessions was in charge from 1987-1993, when he was forced to resign because of ethics complaints; he later worked as a private attorney for, as Unger mentioned earlier, Semion Mogilevich. (Seriously: *the FBI Director left the Bureau to work for the head of the Russian mob.* That's something that really happened!) Sessions' replacement, Louis Freeh, has not been a paragon of squeaky clean in his post-FBI dealings. Then came Mueller, and after Mueller, Comey, whose 2016 decision to disclose the investigation into Clinton but *not* the investigation into Trump cost HRC the election.

And now we have Christopher Wray, a guy Trump appointed *after firing the guy investigating him.* He probably figured that Wray—the attorney who hid Chris Christie's cell phone during Bridgegate and who worked for years at a small private law firm whose main client was Gazprom, Russia's state energy company—would look the other way at his crimes.

IT WAS NOT UNTIL February or March of 2016, Yuri Shvets believes, that the Russians realized Trump had a shot at winning the election. This is when Paul Manafort was hired by the campaign—or, rather, when broke-ass Paul Manafort began to work for the campaign for free. One of Manafort's trusted colleagues was Konstantin Kilimnik, identified by the Senate Intelligence Committee as a Russian intelligence officer who specialized in election fuckery. Per Volume 5, Manafort shared polling data with Kilimnik.

Once Manafort was on board, *that's* when Trump surrogates began meeting with Russians who had close ties to Putin: Sergei Kislyak, the Russian ambassador to the United States; Dimitri Simes, who helped organize the campaign's first foreign policy campaign event at the Mayflower Hotel; Sergei Gorkov, head of VEB, the Russian state bank on the U.S. sanctions list; and Natalia Veselnitskya, the attorney who led the Russian delegation at the Trump Tower meeting of June 9, 2016. (I covered all of this extensively in *Dirty Rubles*.)

And this is not QAnon-of-the-left conspiracy theory—unless you believe the Office of the Special Counsel and the bipartisan Senate Select Committee on Intelligence are putting out disinformation. The frequent, fishy communication between Trump's people and the Russians is confirmed in both the Mueller Report and Volume 5.

"This is what collusion looks like," the latter concludes.

NOTHING ABOUT TRUMP'S TERM as president suggests he turned his back on organized crime upon entering the White House—and certainly not after leaving it. He hasn't "gone legit." While in office, his Twitter antagonists, as discussed, comprised a "Who's Who" of the FBI's Russian mob experts. He routinely attacks the credibility of those who know what he really is.

After he was fired, McCabe began his statement thus: "I have been an FBI Special Agent for over 21 years. I spent half of that time investigating Russian Organized Crime as a street agent and Supervisor in New York City." Why did he stress his experience investigating the Russian mob?

In his book *Higher Loyalty*, James Comey compared Trump to Gravano. "The [loyalty] demand was like

Sammy the Bull's Cosa Nostra induction ceremony—
with Trump in the role of the family boss asking me
if I have what it takes to be a 'made man.'" Of all the
famous mafiosos, why did Comey choose Gravano, a
relatively obscure figure, as the analog?

Gravano himself was asked about the Comey
pull-quote by Jerry Capeci of *Gangland News*; he said,
"The country doesn't need a bookworm as president, it
needs a mob boss. You don't need a Harvard graduate
to deal with these people…[Putin, Kim, Xi] are real
gangsters. You need a fucking gangster to deal with
these people."

So: according to no less an authority on organized
crime than *Sammy the Bull*, Trump is a "mob boss" and
a "fucking gangster."

Okay, then.

Trump is a criminal. That's what he is, what he always
has been, and what he always will be. The four indictments against him, the fraud case in New York that
cost him $500 million, the defamation lawsuit against
his rape victim: these are not products of some Deep
State, Soros-backed conspiracy. It's just a lifetime of
criminality finally catching up to him.

III

JUSTICE UNDONE
An End Run Around the Judicial Process

The Argument: Trump exchanged pardons for loyalty—and, possibly, for money.

As a CRIMINAL, Trump is most comfortable in the presence of other criminals. Other than when he was joking around with the corrupt Russian diplomats in the Oval Office, has he ever looked as happy as he appeared in that video where he's with Jeffrey Epstein, dancing?

Even as the GOP nominee for president in 2016, his inner circle was honeycombed with sketchy characters:

Mike Flynn, his disgraced former national security adviser, is a felon. He was convicted of lying to the FBI. And he was a key figure in the lead-in to January 6,[18]

Michael Cohen, his personal attorney, was convicted of tax evasion and campaign finance violations relating to the Stormy Daniels imbroglio.

Paul Manafort, chair of the Trump campaign from June through August 2016—prime treason season—was indicted for conspiracy against the United States, money laundering, FARA violations, and a host of other charges. He was convicted and spent 23 months in prison.

Roger Stone, Trump's longtime chum and political adviser, was indicted on five counts of false statements, one count of witness tampering, and one count of obstructing an official proceeding. He was convicted and sentenced to 40 months in federal prison.

Stephen K. Bannon, who ran the Trump campaign after Manafort's departure and was even *on the national security team* for a minute, was indicted for wire fraud and money laundering. He was indicted again this past year for obstruction of Congress, and was convicted. He was sentenced to jail time but as of this writing, has yet to be ordered to the hoosegow. The wire fraud trial is ongoing.

George Papadopoulos, one of Trump's foreign policy advisers, was convicted of making false statements to the FBI. His drunken gossip is what led the FBI to open its investigation into Trump's ties to Russia. He served 12 days in federal prison.

---

[18]   Flynn also did a short stint in the clink when he was 17 years old, the seriousness of which charges he tries to minimize in his memoir. I suppose the criminal impulse never quite goes away for some people—rather like riding a bike.

Tom Barrack, a longtime Trump crony and one of his money men, was indicted for acting as an unregistered agent for the UAE. He was acquitted.

Rudy Giuliani—whose father did time in Sing-Sing for sticking up a milkman, and later worked as a mob enforcer—was allegedly involved in the extortion of Ukraine president Zelensky, was a leader of the movement to illegally overturn the 2020 election, and on January 6, 2021, demanded "trial by combat." He was indicted in elections cases in Georgia and Arizona. According to a lawsuit filed against him by a former employee, he is a serial sexual assailant—an allegation that rings true to anyone who saw the second *Borat* movie.

That's a *lot* of shady characters to be associated with—and this is far from a comprehensive list. I haven't mentioned Allen Weisselberg, the longtime CFO of the Trump Organization, who pleaded guilty to 15 felony counts of tax evasion. Or Junior, Eric, and Ivanka. Or Kellyanne Conway's grandfather. Or Matt Gaetz. Or Jim Jordan. Or Erik Prince. Or Eddie Gallagher. Or Ghislaine Maxwell. I did mention Jeffrey Epstein, but still: *Jeffrey Epstein*!

On and on it goes to infinity, a Möbius strip of mountebanks and scoundrels.

To state the obvious: *People don't associate with so many criminals who are not criminals themselves.*

As president, Trump had a singular way of ensuring the loyalty of his crooked associates: he could make their rap sheets disappear.

UNLIKE MOST OTHER POWERS granted to the President by the Constitution, the power to grant executive clemency is virtually unchecked. Some have argued that because the power to grant clemency is unlimited,

Congress has no oversight role over grants of executive clemency. The opposite is true. Because the President can grant clemency to whomever he wants for whatever reasons, it is critically important that certain grants of clemency be subject to Congressional and public scrutiny. If this scrutiny were not applied to grants of clemency, the power could easily be abused.

If the preceding paragraph doesn't sound like my voice, it's because someone else wrote it: Dan Burton, then the chair of the House Committee on Government Reform, and his team. Burton, a Republican, is a former Representative from the 5th District of Indiana. That excerpt is from a lengthy report sent to House Speaker Dennis Hastert on May 14, 2001, entitled "Justice Undone: Clemency Decisions in the Clinton White House," and concerns President Clinton, on his last day in office, granting a pardon to uber-wealthy financiers and longtime international fugitives Marc Rich and Pincus "Pinky" Green.

The pair were indicted on September 19, 1983, on a whopping 65 counts related to tax evasion, mail fraud, racketeering, defrauding the government, and "trading with the enemy." This is what the *New York Times* had to say at the time:

> Marc Rich, one of the world's leading commodity traders, was indicted yesterday by a Federal grand jury on charges that he and a partner had evaded $48 million in income taxes. Prosecutors said it was the biggest tax-fraud indictment in history.

> The two men were also accused of buying oil from Iran after trade with that nation had been declared illegal in response to the Nov. 4, 1979, seizure of American hostages.

> Mr. Rich, a reclusive multimillionaire, and his
> partner, Pincus Green, were charged with 51 counts
> of tax evasion, racketeering and fraud. Through
> a spokesman, both men declared themselves
> innocent.

As soon as he got wind of the prosecution, Rich
turned tail and fled the country, holing up in Switzerland,
a country with a notoriously lax attitude towards foreign
tax collection that he knew would not extradite him. He
spent 17 years on the lam, evading numerous attempts at
arrest—which is no doubt easier to manage if you have
hundreds of millions of dollars to throw at the problem.

Marc Rich was the prototype for an emerging strain
of white-collar criminal that Americans four decades
later know too well. He was amoral, willing to do business with anyone and everyone with the means to engage
his services, no matter how despicable: mobsters, des-
pots, drug traffickers, arms dealers, oligarchs, ayatollahs.
He had no national loyalty; born in Belgium but a U.S.
citizen, he was all too happy to renounce, at the first
whiff of trouble, citizenship of the country that took him
in during the war. He played the intelligence services
of other countries to curry favor with the nation that
issued his passport. And, oh yeah, it was his audacious
cheating on his taxes—which is screwing over the rest
of us—that got him in trouble in the first place. We see
traces of Marc Rich in Paul Manafort, in Roger Stone,
in Jeffrey Epstein, in Jared Kushner, in Erik Prince, in
Donald Trump.

Here is how Burton and the Committee characterized the decision:

> The pardons of Marc Rich and Pincus Green
> were the most controversial and most outrageous

pardons issued by President Clinton, and likely, by any President. Rich and Green were fugitives from justice, and were two of the largest tax cheats in U.S. history. In addition, they had a long and disgraceful record of trading with America's enemies, helping prop up the Ayatollah Khomeini, Saddam Hussein, Muammar Qaddafi, and the Russian mafia, among others. This track record has led even Marc Rich's lawyers to call him a "traitor" and observe that he has "spit on the American flag."

It is beyond any dispute that Marc Rich and Pincus Green did not deserve pardons. Therefore, the inevitable question is why the President granted them . . .

Some of Marc Rich's vast fortune wound up in the hands of his ex-wife, Denise Rich, and through her, to the Democratic Party, the Clinton Presidential Library Foundation, and the Senate campaign of Hillary Clinton. More found its way to Israel, where prominent government officials from across the political spectrum lobbied Bill Clinton on Rich's behalf. Still more was used to pay for fancy lawyers with fancier political connections. The optics were terrible. Whatever President Clinton's actual reasons for granting the pardon, it *looked* sketchy as all get-out. And it reinforced the "crooked Hillary" narrative in 2016—when, a few days before the election, the FBI dumped a tranche of documents related to the Rich pardon.

It's hard to find anyone in Washington, of either party, who supported the move. Democrats were outspoken in their disgust:

Sen. Chuck Schumer: "There can be no justification in pardoning a fugitive from justice. Pardoning a fugitive stands our justice system on its head and makes a mockery of it." (The precedent for not pardoning fugitives dates back to the first Adams Administration.)

Rep. Barney Frank: "It was a real betrayal by Bill Clinton of all who had been strongly supportive of him to do something this unjustified. It was contemptuous."

Rep. Elijah Cummings: "It's one thing to go to trial. It's one thing to stay here and face the music. It's one thing to be found not guilty. It's a whole other thing, in my opinion, when somebody, because they have the money, can go outside the country and evade the system. I tell you it really concerns me because my constituents have a major problem with that, and I do, too."

Rep. Henry Waxman: "The Rich pardon is bad precedent. It appears to set a double standard for the wealthy and powerful. And it is an end run around the judicial process."

Bill Clinton came to regret it, too.

Burton's Committee, meanwhile, positively excoriated the move:

> President Clinton is ultimately responsible for the pardons, and must ultimately provide an explanation of why he granted them. He has, however, failed to provide any satisfactory rationale for his actions. He has failed to answer any serious questions, and instead, has offered only one self-serving, factually inaccurate newspaper column to justify the pardons. President Clinton's attempted explanations have raised more questions than answers about his motivations for granting two of the most unjustified pardons in U.S. history.

> Regardless of the motivations for the Rich and Green pardons, the nation must live with the

consequences of them. The pardons have sent two equally destructive messages. First, by granting the pardons, President Clinton undermined the efforts of U.S. law enforcement to apprehend fugitives abroad. By pardoning a man who evaded capture by the U.S. Marshals Service for almost two decades, President Clinton sent the message that indeed, crime can pay, and that it may be worthwhile to remain a fugitive rather than face charges. The pardon also could undermine U.S. efforts to obtain extradition of fugitives from foreign countries. When a man like Rich can go from the Justice Department's most wanted to a free man with a stroke of the pen, it is difficult for the U.S. to credibly demand the extradition of wanted fugitives. Finally, the pardons send the message that President Clinton did believe that different rules applied to wealthy criminals. If he did not have the money to hire [the well-connected attorney] Jack Quinn and his White House access, Marc Rich never would have obtained a pardon. The President abused one of his most important powers, meant to free the unjustly convicted or provide forgiveness to those who have served their time and changed their lives. Instead, he offered it up to wealthy fugitives whose money had already enabled them to permanently escape American justice. Few other abuses could so thoroughly undermine public trust in government.

Refreshing, isn't it, to remember that Republicans were once capable of moral clarity?

Marc Rich was, without question, a loathsome human who did not deserve his pardon. But here's what Marc Rich *didn't* do: He didn't work with the Kremlin to help his preferred candidate win a presidential election. He didn't share voting data with a Russian intelligence officer who was his business partner. He didn't send Twitter DMs to Russian hackers. He didn't cozy up to Chinese fraudsters to fund his attempts to take down the government. He didn't monetize and politicize a pandemic that got a million Americans killed. He didn't disseminate known lies about stolen elections. He didn't champion insurrection. He wasn't a co-conspirator in one of the worst crimes ever perpetrated in this country. He didn't auction off pardons to the highest bidder.

Bill Clinton pardoning Marc Rich was bad. Donald Trump pardoning Paul Manafort, Roger Stone, Steve Bannon, Mike Flynn, and his other cronies busted by Robert Mueller is orders of magnitude worse. Those pardons were categorically *not* "meant to free the unjustly convicted or provide forgiveness to those who have served their time and changed their lives." On the contrary, all of those men were *emboldened* by their pardons.

Burton's Committee was right that the Rich pardon "undermined the efforts of U.S. law enforcement to apprehend fugitives abroad." By issuing pardons to his criminal pals, Trump undermined the efforts of U.S. law enforcement to *enforce the law*. Those pardons were a giant middle finger to the very concept of justice.[19]

But those are just the most notable pardons. There are plenty of under-the-radar examples of Trump brazenly flaunting the spirit of the presidential pardon in ways that would have made Dan Barton lose his mind.

---

[19]   A little bit of irony: If there's one person who should have been infuriated at the Marc Rich pardon, and who should therefore fundamentally detest the prospect of the hard work of law enforcement going poof with the stroke of a corrupt president's pen, it is Rudolph W. Giuliani. After all, he was the federal prosecutor who indicted Rich in 1983.

On January 19, 2021, the last full day of his presidency, Donald Trump issued a flurry of pardons. Among the beneficiaries was Ken Kurson, a writer, editor, political consultant, and former punk musician.

As pardon material, Kurson was an unorthodox choice. Typically, individuals who receive pardons distinguish themselves by putting their life of crime behind them, by expressing remorse, by giving back to the community, by visibly changing their lives for the better. These are supposed to be redemption stories. There's usually some well-placed senator, governor, or House representative lobbying for the pardon. Sometimes they've already served a big chunk of their prison term; sometimes they've already been out of jail for years.

Kurson was none of those things. He was under indictment for cyberstalking and harassment. The arrest warrant summarizes the nasty, vindictive behavior:

> FBI Special Agents obtained information indicating that KURSON had used the mail, interactive computer services, electronic communication services, electronic communication systems of interstate commerce and other facilities of interstate commerce to stalk and harass Individual No. 1, Individual No. 2 and Individual No. 3 (collectively, the "Victims") between approximately November 2015 and December 2015 . . . . [D]uring this time period, KURSON was engaged in divorce proceedings and blamed Individual No. 1, among others, for the dissolution of his marriage. As a result, beginning in or about November 2015, KURSON threatened to ruin Individual No. 1's reputation and engaged in a pattern of stalking and harassment against Individual No. 1.

There was no respected elder statesman sponsoring the push to Free Kurson. His case *hadn't even gone to trial* when he scored the pardon, so his victims were denied their day in court. And an acquittal was unlikely. The FBI had him dead to rights.

But Kurson had an ace in the hole: he was close friends with Jared Kushner, Trump's son-in-law. Kushner had hired Kurson to head the *New York Observer*, the venerable and beloved Gotham periodical he bought and ruined.[20]

Kurson was also tight with Rudy Giuliani, with whom he'd co-authored a book, and whose ill-fated 2008 presidential campaign he'd worked on. And he'd authored a speech for FPOTUS. In fact, it was Trump's decision to nominate him for a seat on the board of the National Endowment for the Humanities, and the subsequent FBI investigation that followed, that dredged all this up—kind of like what happened to Bernie Kerik, another beneficiary of a Trump pardon, after Bush II sought to nominate him to head Homeland Security.

This means that Kurson was 1) in with Trump, the ultimate arbiter of who got a pardon; 2) BFFs with Kushner; and 3) close to Giuliani. This is like George leaning on his friendship with Paul and his close working relationship with Ringo to score a pardon from John. *Of course* Kurson got his "Get Out of Jail Free" card, just like Kerik did. Charles Kushner, Jared's felon old man, got one, too.

---

[20]   From his own website: "At the Observer, Kurson personally broke dozens of stories, including unearthing audio of Hillary Clinton proposing to rig the 2006 Palestinian Elections [and] a campaign by Samsung to undermine activist investor Elliott Management [note: the company of Paul Singer, of Sam Alito fishing trip fame] that resulted in Congressional inquiry and a change in Samsung policy. . . ."

This is egregiously corrupt—but it gets worse. Guess who was devoting his full attention to presidential pardons in January of 2021 (boldface mine)? This exchange is from the January 6th Committee hearing:

> **Liz Cheney**: "Jared, are you aware of instances where [White House counsel] Pat Cipollone threatened to resign?

> **Jared Kushner**: "I — I kind of — like I said, **my interest at that time was on trying to get as many pardons done**. And I know that, you know, he was always to — him and the team were always saying, 'Oh, we're going to resign. We're not going to be here if this happens, if that happens.' So I kind of took it up to just be whining, to be honest with you."

Then there is the revelation buried in the lawsuit filed last year against the odious Rudy Giuliani by his former employee, Noelle Dunphy. Here are the two relevant paragraphs:

> 132. [Giuliani] also asked Ms. Dunphy if she knew anyone in need of a pardon, telling her that he was selling pardons for $2 million, which he and President Trump would split. He told Ms. Dunphy that she could refer individuals seeking pardons to him, so long as they did not go through "the normal channels" of the Office of the Pardon Attorney, because correspondence going to that office would be subject to disclosure under the Freedom of Information Act.

and

119. To bolster his claims about the need to keep Ms. Dunphy's employment "secret," Giuliani told Ms. Dunphy about other schemes he undertook to reduce the amounts he owed to his ex-wife. For example, Giuliani told Ms. Dunphy that someone owed him $1 million, but Giuliani hinted that instead of having the money paid to him, he had his friend, Robert Stryk, hold it for him. He said, "Robert Stryk just got me a million-dollar payment." This statement was recorded.

It may be that Giuliani was drunk out of his mind, making shit up to impress Dunphy. But if there's any truth to Rudy's bluster—and from what I've heard, this was *not* taken as a joke by the people around him; the scuttlebutt is that he was dead serious—*selling* pardons for $2,000,000 a pop, while not explicitly prohibited by Article II, is pretty clearly a no-no. Remember, it was a crime akin to peddling pardons—attempting to sell off a Senate seat—that took down former Illinois governor Rod Blagojevich. Coincidentally, Blagojevich was 1) a member of Burton's Committee, and 2) himself the recipient of a Trump pardon.

One last note about Ken Kurson: he wasn't able to avoid further legal troubles. Just seven months after scoring his pardon from Trump, he was arrested again. He subsequently pleaded guilty to two misdemeanors related to his cyberstalking.

GIVEN WHAT WE KNOW about Donald Trump's penchant for monetizing anything of value—his endorsement, his TV shows, the Washington hotel he illegally owned while in the White House, the documents he stole—as well as the specificity of Giuliani's instructions, there is little reason to believe Rudy was lying. Put it this way:

If we find out that Trump really *was* selling pardons, would anyone be surprised? Nothing would be more on brand.

Three-plus years later, and in light of Noelle Dunphy's bombshell allegation, it is instructive to look back on the Trump pardons: who got them, what they did to run afoul of the law, and, in the case of his pardoned co-conspirators, what they've been up to since winning their freedom.

Let's start with who Trump chose *not* to pardon. His personal attorney Michael Cohen, who flipped on him, was not pardoned. Jeffrey Epstein was only in custody for six weeks before his death, so he never got a pardon. Ghislaine Maxwell was the beneficiary of a Trump well-wish, but not a pardon. Julian Assange was not pardoned. Edward Snowden was not pardoned. Yevgeny Prigozhin, Putin's chef who Mueller indicted, was not pardoned. Semion Mogilevich was not pardoned. There are some lines, apparently, that even Trump dared not cross.

We should also acknowledge, in the interest of fairness, that some of his pardons were completely justified. I question Trump's motives for pardoning the boxer Jack Johnson or the women's rights leader Susan B. Anthony, but it's for the good that they were formally pardoned. Michael Tedesco was already pardoned by President Obama, but a clerical error didn't absolve him of *all* his crimes; Trump fixed that. And: free Lil Wayne!

The individuals Trump did pardon, in the main, fall into several categories: corrupt members of Congress, most of them Republicans; GOP political operatives; wealthy folks he or his family knew well, or who donated big bucks to his campaign; war criminals; garrulous, bootlicking sycophants; and co-conspirators in his various illicit enterprises, especially related to the 2016 election.

Corrupt Members of Congress

Among the miscreants Trump pardoned were seven former GOP Congressmen: **Chris Collins** of New York (insider trading, lying to the FBI); **Duncan Hunter** of California (conspiracy, wire fraud, campaign finance violations); Texas's **Steve Stockman** (money laundering, misuse of campaign contributions); **Rick Renzi** of Arizona (corruption); North Carolina's **Robin Hayes** (lying to the FBI); **Mark Siljander** of Michigan (obstruction of justice, acting as an unregistered foreign agent; indicted for money laundering); and perhaps the most brazenly corrupt of all, **Duke Cunningham** of California (bribery, fraud, tax evasion).

By issuing the pardons to this motley gaggle of politician crooks, Trump was communicating that it's okay to run financial scams—and break the law in other ways, too—as long as you're a pro-Trump Republican. Hold that thought in your head, and then recall that in late 2020/early 2021, six MAGA Republicans—some of Trump's closest House allies—reportedly requested pardons from FPOTUS: **Mo Brooks, Matt Gaetz, Andy Biggs, Louie Gohmert, Scott Perry**, and the *bête noire* of polite society, **Marjorie Taylor Greene**.

Why would they make such a request? And why would Trump not honor it?

GOP Political Operatives

On the list of Trump pardons are a number of Republican political operatives who had run afoul of the law:

Elliott Broidy, a deputy RNC finance chairman during the Trump campaign, pleaded guilty to working as unregistered foreign agent; he had "sought to lobby the highest levels of the U.S. government to drop one of the largest fraud and money laundering prosecutions ever brought"—involving 1Malaysia Development Berhad (1MDB), a strategic investment and development company wholly owned by the Government of Malaysia—"and to deport a critic of the Chinese Communist Party, all the while concealing the foreign interests whose bidding he was doing," according to a senior DOJ official.

Paul Erickson, famous for being the cuckolded boyfriend of Russian operative Maria Butina, was convicted of wire fraud and money laundering, bilking investors of over a million bucks—what Trump called "a minor financial crime."

Jesse Benton, a longtime aide to both Ron and Rand Paul—and the husband of the former's granddaughter—was convicted of "conspiring to solicit and cause an illegal campaign contribution by a foreign national, effecting a conduit contribution, and causing false records to be filed with the FEC," per the DOJ. He *took money from Russia and diverted what he didn't take for himself to Trump.*

Ed Henry, state chair of Trump's campaign in Alabama and a former lawmaker, was convicted of healthcare fraud.

Dinesh D'Souza, the rightwing media figure best known for his Big Lie propaganda film *2000 Mules*, was convicted of campaign finance fraud.

All of these dudes got pardoned.

Co-Conspirators

Trump was loyal to those who showed him loyalty, gamely pardoning those convicted co-conspirators who did *not* turn on him:

Paul Manafort, among many other treasonous things, gave election data to a Russian intelligence officer who specialized in election rigging. He left prison early because of covid, and then got a full pardon. He'd been pretty quiet since—until March of this year, when Trump floated the idea of bringing him back to the campaign.

George Papadopoulos has been busy promoting the book he wrote about his experiences. Otherwise, he too has been quiet.

But not **Steve Bannon**. He's a fount of disinformation via his *War Zone* podcast. After the pardon, he was convicted of contempt of Congress, and as of this writing, we're still waiting for him to see the inside of a jail cell. Another criminal trial, about the corrupt fundraiser to Build the Wall, also looms.

Had they not secured pardons from Trump—*they* didn't have to sweat it out until the last possible moment; their pardons were *prioritized*—**Roger Stone** and **Mike Flynn** may have been in prison in January 2021, instead of in the thick of the insurrection activity. Pardoning Roger Stone is like fertilizing a tumor. Pardoning General Flynn is like freeing General Zod. No good can possibly come of it.

There's also Sheriff Joe Arpaio, and Trump's well-heeled pal Conrad Black, and the art dealer Helly Nahmad, who ran an illegal gambling operation *at Trump Tower.*

Taken together, these are the kind of people a president of Russia or Belarus or Uzbekistan might pardon. The takeaway is obvious: if you go to bat for Trump, don't worry about prison; he's got your back. How can his indicted manservant Waltine Nauta look at all the Trump pardonees and not rest assured that his employer and protector will pardon *him*, too, if Trump winds up getting another term? Should FPOTUS become POTUS, he has promised to pardon the worst of the worst, including anyone convicted of crimes related to January 6. Every Capitol besieger, including the leaders of the Proud Boys—who were convicted of seditious conspiracy and received long prison sentences—will be set free, with zero incentive not to exact revenge.

The Constitution is vague on the subject, but presidential pardons are intended to correct errors or to show mercy, not to reward sycophants for their loyalty, and certainly not to obstruct justice. It is also strongly implied that a president cannot pardon himself.

But then, the Founders assumed the Chief Executive would not himself be a criminal.

IV

PLAGUE & INSURRECTION
Catastrophic failure upon catastrophic failure

The Argument: Trump was a terrible president.

1/ Plague

ON JANUARY 24, 2020, the Centers for Disease Control confirmed a second travel-related infection of the SARS-CoV-2 virus in the United States, this time in Illinois.

The Illinois case was the epidemiological equivalent of the second airplane hitting the World Trade Center. It meant that the first U.S. infection, reported in Washington State four days earlier, was not an isolated incident. It meant that the virus—which WHO would not dub "covid-19" for another month—had come to stay.

It meant that the pandemic was here.

"Ultimately, we expect we will see community spread in this country," Nancy Messonnier said on February 26, 2020, as American passengers on a cruise ship called the *Diamond Princess*, site of an early SARS-CoV-2 outbreak, waited in quarantine off the coast of Japan. "It's not so much a question of *if* this will happen anymore but rather more a question of exactly *when* this will happen and how many people in this country will have severe illness."

At the time, Messonnier was the CDC's incident manager for the covid-19 response. At the time, there were just—but already!—53 confirmed cases on American soil. That jaw-dropping statement was made during a remarkable telebriefing to reporters. She also said this:

> These [non-pharmaceutical interventions] are practical measures that can help limit exposure by reducing exposure in community settings. Students in smaller groups or in a severe pandemic, closing schools and using internet-based teleschooling to continue education. For adults, businesses can replace in-person meetings with video or telephone conferences and increase teleworking options. On a larger scale, communities may need to modify, postpone, or cancel mass gatherings. Looking at how to increase telehealth services and delaying elective surgery.

And this:

Some community-level interventions that may be most effective in reducing the spread of a new virus like school closures are also the most likely to be associated with unwanted consequences and further disruptions. Secondary consequences of some of these measures might include missed work and loss of income. I understand this whole situation may seem overwhelming and that disruption to everyday life may be severe. But these are things that people need to start thinking about now.

And, in response to a reporter's question, this:

You know, diseases surprise us and therefore we need to be reacting to the current situation even if it differs from what we planned for. You know, in general we are asking the American public to work with us to prepare in the expectation that this could be bad. I continue to hope that in the end we'll look back and feel like we are over-prepared, but that is a better place to be in than being under-prepared.

These comments expounded on what she'd said at a controversial White House press briefing the day before—the one that reportedly made President Trump throw the proverbial ketchup.

Nancy Messonnier knows her shit. She was the director of the National Center for Immunization and Respiratory Diseases. She worked on the response to the 2001 anthrax attacks. She helped develop a vaccine to combat meningococcal meningitis, stemming an outbreak in Africa. She's also a military veteran, having served as a captain in the United States Public Health Service Commissioned Corps, and the sister of Rod Rosenstein, Trump's deputy Attorney General. In a

Republican administration especially, she is *exactly* who you want in charge of the federal pandemic response.

But she made the blunder of being a little too good at her job *in an election year*. Rather than heed her advice or listen to her warnings, Donald Trump immediately sidelined her.

The day after the first CDC White House presser—February 26, 2020, the same day Messonnier was taking questions from reporters in the teleconference—Trump named Mike Pence chair of the White House Coronavirus Task Force, replacing Health & Human Services secretary Alex Azar. Pence immediately installed Deborah Birx, a specialist in HIV/AIDS immunology and a U.S. health ambassador, as coronavirus response coordinator—presumably because her forecasts were sunnier than Messonnier's.

Birx and her colorful scarves became the White House's primary covid-19 messenger. Messonnier, the SARS-CoV-2 oracle, went dark. But as anyone familiar with Greek lore can tell you, ignoring the sibyl's prophesies doesn't make them not come true.

THE WHITE HOUSE'S ROSY covid-19 messaging was especially mendacious because privately, President Trump agreed with Messonnier's assessment. Early in February, he told the reporter Bob Woodward, "This is deadly stuff . . . . You just breathe the air, and that's how it's passed. And so that's a very tricky one. That's a very delicate one. It's also more deadly than even your strenuous flu."

Publicly, however, Trump downplayed the threat. "This is a flu," he told White House reporters on February 27. "This is like a flu." He kept up with this "flu" narrative—which he'd known all along was total horseshit (see Chapter 1). On March 9, 2020, he tweeted: "So last year 37,000 Americans died from the common Flu. It averages between 27,000 and 70,000 per year. Nothing is shut down, life & the economy go on. At this moment there are 546 confirmed cases of CoronaVirus, with 22 deaths. Think about that!"

When the President of the United States repeatedly claims that a new virus is no big whoop, the American people—even people in the other party; even a pathological liar like Donald—assume he's telling the truth. But Trump was not telling the truth. He was lying. And he knew it.

Caught in the lie when Woodward's book *Rage* (finally) came out six months and two hundred thousand covid deaths later, Trump explained that he was merely trying to avoid panic. "We have to show calm," he told reporters in September of 2020, echoing the strategy of George W. Bush 19 Septembers previously. "Certainly I'm not going to drive this country or the world into a frenzy. We want to show confidence. We have to show strength." But it is one thing to avoid panic, quite another to willfully, cynically lie about matters of life and death.

The ugly truth is that Trump recognized early on that covid-19 could bring about the end of his presidency, so he decided to prioritize his own political fortunes over public health. By disseminating disinformation, demonizing experts, deriding masks, blaming Democrats for every failure—in short, by *politicizing the pandemic response*—he sacrificed voters for votes.

Bottom line: to help himself win re-election, Trump allowed people to die.

THE BRAINS BEHIND THE DECISION to let the virus ravage the blue states of New York, New Jersey, and California—where the first big U.S. outbreaks occurred—belonged to Trump's ghoulish son-in-law, Jared Kushner.

As Katherine Eban revealed in her damning *Vanity Fair* piece of July 30, 2020, Kushner, tasked by Trump in March 2020 to figure out a plan for the federal pandemic response, formed a team of "Morgan Stanley bankers liaising with billionaires," a group that included his college roommate, to tackle the problem. None of them had a background in public health. By some miracle, the team managed to devise a workable plan that called for aggressive, widespread, centralized testing—only to have it go "poof into thin air" in April, as one participant told Eban. She writes:

> President Trump had been downplaying concerns about the virus and spreading misinformation about it—efforts that were soon amplified by Republican elected officials and right-wing media figures. Worried about the stock market and his reelection prospects, Trump also feared that more testing would only lead to higher case counts and more bad publicity. Meanwhile, Dr. Deborah Birx, the White House's coronavirus response coordinator, was reportedly sharing models with senior staff that optimistically—and erroneously, it would turn out—predicted the virus would soon fade away.

> Against that background, the prospect of launching a large-scale national plan was losing favor, said one public health expert in frequent contact with the White House's official coronavirus task force.

> Most troubling of all, perhaps, was a sentiment the expert said a member of Kushner's team expressed:

that because the virus had hit blue states hardest, a national plan was unnecessary and would not make sense politically. "The political folks believed that because it was going to be relegated to Democratic states, that they could blame those governors, and that would be an effective political strategy," said the expert.

That logic may have swayed Kushner. "It was very clear that Jared was ultimately the decision maker as to what [plan] was going to come out," the expert said.

By the end of April 2020, with the covid death toll at a then-staggering 62,557—more than the lives lost in Vietnam and some 20 times the number of people who perished on 9/11—the die had been cast. Kushner rolled out his plan for mass death. Trump signed off on it. Mike Pence, nominally in charge of the pandemic task force, did nothing to stop it.

And Trump merrily continued to pump lies into the discourse, even when he himself took ill from covid, and almost died, a month before the 2020 election—by which day almost a quarter million Americans would be dead from covid-19. Pence rarely made his presence felt. Birx continued to downplay the danger. Kushner was so dead-set on his plan of mass extermination that *even during the transition*, with the election over and lost, he refused to turn over information about covid planning to the incoming Biden team.

And all that time, people continued get sick, people continued to be hospitalized, and people continued to die.

PLAGUES HAPPEN from time to time. There is no question that covid-19 was going to spread to the United

States, sure as it spread to every other country on earth. But there is also no question that the willful negligence of Trump and Kushner—with a big assist from the media empire of Rupert Murdoch, one of the very first humans to get vaccinated, despite his Fox News anchors spreading fatal disinformation about the vaccines— exacerbated the pandemic. How many American lives would have been spared, had Trump and Kushner not poured gasoline on the SARS-CoV-2 fire?

As a University of Connecticut study determined,

> the U.S. COVID-19 mortality rate for 2020, adjusted for population, was more than twice as high as Canada's and Germany's; ten times higher than India's; 29 times higher than Australia's; 40 times higher than Japan's; 59 times higher than South Korea's, and 207 times higher than New Zealand's mortality rate. In fact, U.S. performance at the level of South Korea, Australia, New Zealand, or Japan in containing the pandemic would have saved over 300,000 American lives in 2020 alone.

That is inexcusable. That is gross negligence on the grandest possible scale. It's so horrifying it boggles the mind.

By January 24, 2023, more Americans had died from covid-19 (1,099,866) than lost their lives in the Revolutionary War, the Civil War, and World War II combined (1,091,399). That's a staggering number—far greater than the entire population of San Francisco, Seattle, Austin, Denver, Boston, Detroit, or Washington. And those are just the deaths the CDC knew about. The actual figure was certainly much higher.

In a press conference on March 26, 2020, Deborah Birx pooh-poohed a model suggesting that 60 million

Americans would be infected by covid-19. Three years later, there were over a hundred million infections that the CDC knew about; the real number was significantly higher, likely more than twice the figure that so troubled the bescarfed Birx back then.

And I'm only talking about life and death here, not the vast spaces in between. Not everyone who comes down with SARS-CoV-2 makes a full recovery. We can only guess at the long-term effects of infection. Long covid is real, and we will have to contend with it for generations to come.

Three years after the second covid diagnosis in the United States, FPOTUS was the eulogist at the funeral of a longtime supporter: Diamond, of Diamond & Silk fame. She was an unvaccinated professional liar who was rumored to have died of covid-19—the same virus that killed Herman Cain and a bevy of rightwing radio hosts. How did Trump's potential complicity in her death not come up in all the reporting of the funeral?

"I think if we didn't do what we did, we'd have had millions die," Trump told Woodward in the late winter of 2020.

He had it backwards. In actuality, *because* they did what they did, more than a million *have* died, including almost 400,000 by the time he left office.

2/ Insurrection

ON THE SIXTH OF JANUARY 2021, Donald Trump tried to overthrow the government. He incited an insurrection: whipping up his MAGA horde into a frenzy, encouraging them to besiege the Capitol, and watching it all unfold on TV, doing nothing as innocent people died.

It was the worst attack on our democracy since Booth shot Lincoln.

The coup failed, like most things Trump tries. His own cowardice contributed to that failure. The Capitol police held the line. The deranged and hellbent besieger Ashli Babbitt was shot dead, frightening the less committed MAGA. Members of Congress survived unscathed. Mike Pence refused to go along with the scheme. Despite the efforts of Trump's lieutenants and a gaggle of seditious senators, the vote was certified. Even Republican stalwarts like Kevin McCarthy and Mitch McConnell condemned Trump and the insurrection. Justice prevailed.

But things could just as easily have gone south. Pence could have ignored the advice of Dan Quayle and the lecture by his son—or he could have been hanged before he even got to make the call. The besiegers could have been armed with assault rifles and mowed down Capitol police. Nancy Pelosi could have been in her office when it was breached. The pipe bomb outside the Democratic Party headquarters could have exploded while VP-Elect Kamala Harris was inside the building. Trump could have shown up at Capitol Hill to heroically lead his MAGA army, instead of cravenly watching the events unfold on cable news.

The truth is, we got lucky.

To mark the third anniversary of the failed insurrection earlier this year, I went back and looked at some of the pieces I'd written in January of 2021. Time has a way of mellowing our feelings about that emotionally charged event—especially if you're a Republican who was in the Capitol that day—and I was curious what I'd been thinking in the heat of the moment. At the time, my primary concern was that Trump be impeached and removed immediately, before he could further damage the country; we got the former but not the latter, and are still paying the price.

My first January 2021 piece, "Trump and Punishment," a meditation on the aforementioned John Wilkes Booth and traitors, includes this excerpt:

> Andrew Johnson's failure to properly punish the traitors—and make no mistake: Robert E. Lee, Jefferson Davis, and their Confederates were all stinking traitors, the vilest in American history— has ripple effects to this day. There is a thruline from the half-assed Reconstruction to Ford pardoning Nixon, and from there to Obama not investigating Bush and Cheney for war crimes.

> This is what we do in this country. We repeat the same mistake, over and over and over. We let the bad guys off the hook. The traitors. The murderers. The thieves. The confidence men. The so-called "white collar" criminals. All escape with a slap on the wrist. And if history is our guide, that's exactly what will happen to the despotic Donald John Trump and his gaggle of venal collaborators—some of whom he has already pardoned!

> We cannot—we must not—allow that to happen. The crimes are too serious, the damage to the country and the world too great. For the soul of the nation to survive, we must recognize the crimes of the President and his co-conspirators for what they are: a coordinated attack on our democracy. Trump's attempt to extort the Georgia Secretary of State to steal the election is only the most recent in a long line of examples.

It's difficult to wrap our minds around this, I'll allow. *This* level of sedition, practiced by *this many* politicians, has not been seen in this country since the 1860s.

What's notable is that I wrote that on January 5, 2021—the day *before* the insurrection. I was already convinced that Trump was a clear and present danger to our democracy.

Was he ever!

THE FIRST PREVAIL PIECE *after* the insurrection, "Trump Crusaders, On the March," posted on January 8, 2021. By then, I had moved beyond the 1860s and had the turn of the 13th century on the brain:

> What we now know as the Fourth Crusade began in 1199, when a troop of rough-and-tumble French noblemen—the MAGA of their day—heeded the new Pope's call to liberate the Holy Land from the infidels.

> The endeavor was bankrolled by the Doge of Venice, Enrico Dandolo, who was in his eighties and almost blind—a decrepit mob boss, basically. Using what amounted to early-13th-century psyops, the Doge managed to convince the Frenchmen that *before* they attacked Jerusalem, they should *first* lay siege to Constantinople. This made zero sense to the self-righteous Crusaders, because Constantinople was a Christian city—the seat of the Eastern Orthodox Church. Why should they make war with other Christians? But the Doge needed this to happen: the Byzantine emperor owed him a lot of money, and this was

an excellent opportunity to use borrowed muscle to collect on the debt.

Constantinople was famously impregnable: surrounded by difficult-to-navigate waters on three sides, and defended on the fourth by a series of unscalable walls, of the kind Trump never managed to build. Even Attila the Hun took one look at the place and kept heading West. But in April of 1204, the Doge and his French brute squad managed. They landed their ships on the perilous shore, and the Byzantine guardsmen helped them penetrate the city walls.

Once inside, the Crusaders lay waste to the greatest city in the world, slaughtering its citizens, raping its women, burning its buildings (including the great library), destroying its precious artwork, and stealing whatever they could get their grimy hands on. As one historian put it: "There was never a greater crime against humanity than the Fourth Crusade." That this unspeakable horror was committed in the name of Jesus Christ did not escape the notice of the Pope, who was livid when he heard the news. "Whoever suggested such a thing to you," he wrote, "and how did they lead your mind astray?" The Pope's C.Y.A. tone was similar to Mitch McConnell's on Wednesday night.

Before Trump came along, back when I was still writing fiction, I spent a good year and a half working on a historical novel about the Byzantine Empire. This was a robust civilization that for seven centuries was the center of Medieval Christendom, the cultural capital of the Western world. And now? Most people are only vaguely acquainted with its name. Its greatest contribution to modern society is probably the word *icon*.

When empires fall, they fall fast.

I've thought about the Fourth Crusade a lot these last few days—since the motley MAGA army of smirking cosplay insurrectionists stormed the U.S Capitol. The Constantinopolitans surely knew that the three emperors who held the throne from 1199 to 1204—Alexius III, whom the Doge installed; the Trumpy Alexius IV, who robbed the treasury and fled; Alexius V, the Mike Pence-like sap who was left holding the bag—were bumblers. But I'm sure they did not realize, as they prepared for Easter that fateful year, that their city was on the verge of being destroyed—that life, as they knew it, was over.

The Crusades, and the Fourth Crusade specifically, remain a valid comp. Like the French soldier class of the 11th century, MAGA was susceptible to powerful disinformation campaigns. To this day, the fervor of Trump's most loyal supporters is more religious than logical—which is why common sense, reason, and cogent arguments don't get through to them. Those who believe they're right are always more dangerous than those who think they are. You can't argue with faith.

By January 11, writing in *DAME Magazine*, I was coming to terms with what happened and what should be done about it. Here are the last three paragraphs:

This is what sedition looks like. We throw that word around casually, and Trump's allies overuse it to dilute its effect. But that's what that was. We just experienced a viable attempt by a lame-duck president and his supporters to overthrow the government. Anyone involved with this must be indicted, prosecuted, and punished to the fullest extent of the law.

And that's why impeachment should move forward, even after Trump's term of office ends. After January 20, he will no longer enjoy the protections of the presidency. He will be a private citizen, compelled like the rest of us to testify under oath. That impeachment trial could—and should—function as a commission for the besieging. Call Hawley to the stand, and ask why he saluted the insurrectionists. Call Cruz and ask what prompted him to give that speech. Call Brooks and Boebert. Call Giuliani and grill him like a well-done Mar-a-Lago burger patty. Call Junior and Ivanka and Eric. Call Lin Wood and Mike Flynn and Roger Stone. Call Pence.

After four years of lies, we're due for a bracing dose of truth.

Some of the January 6 planners were indeed convicted of seditious conspiracy, and will be in prison for years to come (unless Trump wins and pardons them, which he will absolutely do, as discussed in the previous chapter). The January 6th Committee did get some of those people on record. But we have yet to hear from Hawley or Cruz or Brooks or Boebert or Giuliani or Wood or Flynn or Stone or Pence or Trump's three oldest spawn. And, to their great and eternal shame, enough Republican senators voted to acquit the instigator of the greatest attack on our democracy in 16 decades that Trump remains at large: the Republican frontrunner.

THE THIRD OF MY JANUARY 2021 pieces about the insurrection, "Capitol Records," posted on January 15—five days before Biden's inauguration:

> When John Wilkes Booth shot Abraham Lincoln, he exclaimed, "*Sic semper tyrannis.*" That is the state motto of Virginia, and it means, "Thus always to tyrants." Booth fervently believed that the democratically elected President of the United States was a power-mad despot, and that, by killing him, he was liberating his countrymen from tyranny. In his sick mind, he was a hero. In reality, he was an angry white supremacist, radicalized by false grievance: MAGA 1.0. He fell for the Big Lie of the 1860s—just as his spiritual descendants fell for the lie that the 2020 election was stolen from their Führer, Donald John Trump.
>
> I keep referencing the mid-nineteenth century because the Civil War is the only precedent in our nation's history to what's happening right now. "Stupid Watergate," we jokingly called it, but Trump has gone far beyond the wildest excesses of Richard Nixon. The republic is *under attack*—present tense. The peaceful transition of power, which took place even in 1860, is in jeopardy. Troops are bivouacked in the Capitol. The lame-duck president, an inveterate criminal, wants to remain in office, mostly to avoid prosecution. Whether motivated by cynical political calculation, rank delusion, authoritarian radicalism, coercion, or fear for their

family's lives, the lion's share of a once-proud political party—ironically, the Party of Lincoln—has thrown in with him. Republicans failed to remove Trump a year ago; 400,000 Americans are dead because of their failure. Granted a second chance to do the right thing, most of the GOP balked.

Last Wednesday, a coup attempt came a hair's breadth away from succeeding. The collaborators sought to, first, stop the electoral votes from being counted, because Trump had been told, wrongly, that this would prevent Joe Biden from taking office (by the same lousy low-rent lawyer who wrote the Kamala Harris birther attack in *Newsweek!*); and second, hunt down and execute Vice President Mike Pence, House Speaker Nancy Pelosi, and possibly Senate President Pro Tempore Chuck Grassley....Why else were there gallows erected outside? Why else would the Secret Service have whisked Pence away? The besiegers were *seeking out* Mike Pence, and they were *seeking out* Nancy Pelosi—and they made it into the latter's offices, terrorizing her young staffers, smashing her mirror, and making off with her fucking laptop. What do we think these berserkers would have done if they had found her there? Shared a pot of tea? Binged *Downton Abbey*? Quilted?

Again: January 6 was an attempt to do harm to leaders in the presidential line of succession. This is no small thing. It's not something we can gloss over because of "unity." It's the worst attack by secessionists since Lee surrendered. And only by the grace of God, and the heroic acts of police like Eugene Goodman, were we spared a bloodbath.

That coup attempt was instigated by a number of powerful players, including the President, members of his family, his personal attorney, two sitting Senators, a cabal of seditious House Representatives, various and sundry alt-right personalities, and the wife of a sitting Supreme Court Justice. Three sitting Congressmen coordinated with the event's organizer. At least one, Lauren Boebert, tweeted out Pelosi's location during the besieging, directly violating orders by the security detail. The day before, members of Congress allegedly gave a recon tour of the warren of hallways in the Senate to some of the attackers, who came with schematic maps and seemed to know exactly where to go to find key individuals. Even now, with additional security members in place, some gun-happy members of Congress, all vocal supporters of "Stop the Steal," are refusing to walk through metal detectors. Rep. Madison Cawthorn claims he was packing heat during the besieging; given his lusty support of "Stop the Steal," Donald Trump, Adolf Hitler, and firearms, we should be grateful he didn't take out Pelosi himself.

Certainly there were people on the inside with some inkling of what was happening. Ali Alexander, the alt-right dipshit who helped organize the "Stop the Steal" rally, confessed that three members of Congress helped him plan the event: Mo Brooks, Andy Biggs, and Paul Gosar. The remarkable video by the photojournalist Sandi Bachom shows that the attack on the Capitol was well orchestrated; group leaders with megaphones issued commands, which the rank-and-file followed. And the police did not arrive on the scene until it was too late. And here we are.

It took a besieging of the Capitol for Nancy Pelosi to mobilize for a second impeachment. But mobilize she did. Indeed, the House went from being attacked by the MAGA terrorists to voting to impeach the President in less than a week. There are many reasons for pursuing this path to its conclusion, but one of the most obvious is to get the traitors on record. History will show that contemptible scoundrels like Jim Jordan, Matt Gaetz, Devin Nunes, and Elise Stefanik voted to keep the tyrant in power . . . .

The events of January 6 comprised an attack on our republic, the likes of which have not befallen this nation since the Civil War. And the perpetrators of this ghastly crime, this desecration of our sacred space, must not get off lightly . . . .

Me, I hold with these sentiments:

On January 6, 2021 a violent mob attacked the United States Capitol to obstruct the process of our democracy and stop the counting of presidential electoral votes. This insurrection caused injury, death and destruction in the most sacred space in our Republic.

Much more will become clear in coming days and weeks, but what we know now is enough. The President of the United States summoned this mob, assembled the mob, and lit the flame of this attack. Everything that followed was his doing. None of this would have happened without the President. The President could have immediately and forcefully intervened to stop the violence. He did not. There has never been a greater betrayal by a President of the United States of his office and his oath to the Constitution.

I will vote to impeach the President.

The Squad-loving radical socialist member of Congress who wrote those stirring words? Liz Cheney, one of just ten House Republicans who voted to impeach. Strange bedfellows indeed!

Trump is a petty, greedy despot who has egregiously violated, again and again, his promise to defend the United States. Now he has instigated a coup. He must be removed from office, prosecuted for his heinous crimes, and remanded to ADX Florence for the rest of his miserable life.

Thus always to tyrants.

I believed that then, and I believe it now. The only thing that has changed in the last three years is that Trump has *embraced* the role of tyrant, encouraging comparisons to Adolf Hitler (!) and making plans to turn the presidency into a dictatorship (of which more in Chapters 5-7). As such, he's a figure both Lincoln *and* Booth would have reviled.

To summarize what we've covered so far: Donald Trump, an inveterate criminal, won the White House with help from his whoremasters in Russia; lied egregiously to the American people for four years; and exacerbated two of the worst disasters in the nation's history—one of which, January 6, he himself created.

This is a man who should never again be trusted with the keys to the nuclear launch codes—or our classified documents, which he blithely made off with when he left office.

Indeed, according to the Constitution, Trump is ineligible to be POTUS. The Fourteenth Amendment makes it clear that Donald, as the ringleader of the failed insurrection, is prohibited from serving a second term as president. This was written during Reconstruction, after the Civil War. The third clause makes its position on sedition unequivocal:

> No person shall be a Senator or Representative in Congress, or elector of President and Vice-President, or hold any office, civil or military, under the United States, or under any State, who, having previously taken an oath, as a member of Congress, or as an officer of the United States, or as a member of any State legislature, or as an executive or judicial officer of any State, to support the Constitution of the United States, **shall have engaged in insurrection or rebellion against the same**, or given aid or comfort to the enemies thereof. But Congress may by a vote of two-thirds of each House, remove such disability.

But a supine Supreme Court, including three mediocrities selected by Trump himself, have determined that the Fourteenth Amendment does not say what the Fourteenth Amendment says.

Lisa Graves, now the executive director of True North Research, previously served as Deputy Assistant Attorney General in the Office of Policy Development at the Department of Justice, Chief Counsel for Nominations for Senator Patrick Leahy on the U.S.

Senate Judiciary Committee, and Deputy Chief of the Article III Judges Division of the Administrative Office of the U.S. Courts, with oversight of the Financial Disclosure Office. She is an attorney and an expert in this sort of thing. In that decision, Graves told me on my podcast, SCOTUS took it upon itself to "rewrite the Fourteenth Amendment, the third clause of it…to assert that there's a unanimous view on the Court that the Fourteenth Amendment requires an…implementing statute in order to bar someone from office for engaging in insurrection."

This is categorically *not* what the Fourteenth Amendment asserts. "That clause says that people who engage in insurrection are barred from office. And it has one escape clause: Congress, by a two-thirds vote, can remove that impediment. So it's the *opposite* of requiring implementation," she explains. "In fact, the only thing that requires implementation is if you want to *remove* that bar, then two-thirds of Congress have to remove it. And so [the decision] was totally counterfactual, counter-textual. And then it turns out that it wasn't really a unanimous decision on that point. The only unanimity was that they didn't want to let Colorado be the only state, basically, to take Trump from the ballot."

Trump and his "SCOTUS whisperer" Leonard Leo—more on him shortly—have packed our highest court with Justices who will decide that black is white, up is down, or Coldplay is Radiohead, as long as it moves the needle for Donald Trump.

"I don't have any confidence that this Court would stand up to a second Trump administration," Graves tells me. "Or if they managed to—out of some miracle, [if] there were five votes against him on something, that Trump would even follow it—that he would follow any rule against him."

Needless to say, installing friendly judges on the bench, and ignoring their decisions when convenient, is something dictators do. And Trump wants nothing more than to be a dictator.

V

ENTER STRONGMAN
"Trump being Trump" is Trump Being Hitler

The Argument: Trump wants dictatorial powers.

DONALD TRUMP IS A WANNABE strongman. He's an authoritarian at heart. He's the Mussolini of Queens, an American Hitler. Donald Trump does not want to be the 47th President of the United States; Donald Trump wants to be the nation's first dictator.

At this point, no serious commentator doubts this. The neocon dignitary Robert Kagan said as much in a *Washington Post* op-ed in November: "Let's stop the wishful thinking and face the stark reality: There is a clear path to dictatorship in the United States, and it is getting shorter every day."

Mike Godwin, the Godwin who developed Godwin's Law—that is, that "as an online discussion grows longer, the probability of a comparison involving Nazis or Hitler approaches one"—said that it *is* appropriate to compare Trump to Hitler: "[W]hen people draw parallels between Donald Trump's 2024 candidacy and Hitler's progression from fringe figure to Great Dictator, we aren't joking. Those of us who hope to preserve our democratic institutions need to underscore the resemblance before we enter the twilight of American democracy."

Okay, fine, he's a dictator. But what does that *mean*, exactly? Presidents, even weak ones, already have enormous power. So what separates POTUS from strongman? The answer is simple: their relationship to the law. The former are willing to be constrained by it; the latter bend it to serve their own tyrannical purposes. As the rhetoric scholar Jen Mercieca, author of *Demagogue for President*, explains in a recent piece in *Resolute Square*, "When political officials are held accountable to established law, that's called democratic 'rule of law'—the thing that [Sean] Hannity asked Trump if he would violate." She continues:

> But Trump, like all dictators before him, claims that the other side has already broken the rule of law—that the rule of law doesn't exist because his political enemies are cheaters. That claim gives him permission, like all unaccountable leaders before him, to argue that the nation needs a "strong leader" like him who will rid the country of supposed "lawlessness." Trump would rid the nation of "lawlessness" by assuming uncontrollable power.
>
> Would-be dictators don't want to be held accountable to the rule of law themselves because,

obviously, the rule of law restrains their power. Dictators want the law to be arbitrary; they want to have the power to decide which laws will be enforced and who is subject to enforcement and who is not. When political officials apply the rule of law as it suits them and to advance their own interests, that's called autocratic "rule by law."

Trump, in short, doesn't believe that the rules apply to him. *L'État, c'est Donald.*

This isn't a new development. Avoiding consequences for his shitty behavior, we might reasonably say, is, to date, his life's greatest success. He stiffs vendors. He falsifies business records. He steals classified documents. He cheats on his taxes and on his loan applications and on his wives. He rapes with impunity. And he always seems to get away with it.

"Democracy," Mercieca reminds us, "requires that those laws are followed and enforced both for citizens and officials." In Donald's case, that hasn't been happening for some time. Even his indictments seem not to matter.

Trump has already managed to pervert the rule of law in four ways: inexplicable delay in indictment, trial, and punishment; corruption of the judiciary; abuse of the presidential pardon (as previously discussed); and, most ominously, weaponization of law enforcement to attack his enemies. Combined, this undermines our collective faith in the fairness of the legal system—the rock on which is built the church of our state.

Dictator. Fascist. Autocrat. Despot. Tyrant. These are not just labels intended to insult the presumptive GOP presidential candidate. These are not words thrown around casually. Trump really *is* all of those things. Unfortunately, most people don't have the imagination, or the knowledge of history, to understand what this would mean, in practical terms: What would an American dictatorship look like?

In the very short term, it would look like Hungary, where another corpulent Putin puppet with ties to the Russian mob, Viktor Orbán, has set up an "illiberal democracy," with himself as permanent Prime Minister. Voting rights—fairness at the ballot box—will be the first casualty. The rightwing minority will rule, literally. Like a vampire summoned through the window, once Trump is back in the White House, there will be no getting rid of him. Term limits will apply as little as any other law he doesn't approve of; indeed, his disciples are already calling for the Twenty-Second Amendment to be overturned. Then the country will be reconstituted in Russia's image.

"Hungary is an intermediate stop to Russia," the senior defense analyst Brynn Tannehill, author of *American Fascism*, told me. "Hungary is the same as Russia, just ten years behind in terms of the autocratic movement."

In the U.S., there will be no big surprises. The GOP's despotic vision has been laid out in a horrifying Heritage Foundation document, Project 2025's *Mandate for Leadership*, that, as I explain in Chapter 7, would make Sir Oswald Mosely tumesce. Trump has his lieutenants in place this time around—zealots like Stephen Miller, Mike Davis, Kash Patel, and Michael Anton, who are as capable as they are fash.

"Where we are right now is that Donald Trump wants to set himself up as a dictator," Tannehill told me. "They have laid it out very, very clearly in Project 2025's *Mandate for Leadership*. I've tweeted about it, I've written about it. They are being more and more manifestly authoritarian with a goal of reshaping the

United States in ways that would render us unrecognizable in terms of foreign policy, in terms of domestic policy, in terms of making abortion and birth control and healthcare for trans people completely unavailable, illegal. To make it possible for Red States to reach out and grab people they don't like from Blue States to prosecute them."

In short, there will be a war on women's healthcare, contraception, LGBTQ rights, and a lot of the freedoms we take for granted. There will also be state-sanctioned vengeance against anyone who has betrayed Dear Leader. Kash Patel said as much, in his recent appearance on Steve Bannon's podcast:

> We will go out and find the conspirators, not just in government but in the media. Yes, we're going to come after the people in the media who lied about American citizens, who helped Joe Biden rig presidential elections.

> We're going to come after you, whether it's criminal or civilly, we'll figure that out. But yeah, we're putting you all on notice and Steve, this is why they hate us. This is why we're tyrannical. This is why we're dictators.

By "civilly," Patel means through frivolous lawsuits designed to bankrupt their detractors.

And if that weren't enough, there will also be a fatal dose of rightwing Jesus. You know: the Jesus who hates His neighbor as He hates Himself.

"We are looking at a government that is going to elevate one particular brand of Christianity above all others and make it a singular force in both law and public policy," Tannehill says. "These are things that *should* be unacceptable and are going to certainly set off protests, but what we're also seeing is, Trump is talking about invoking the Insurrection Act, clearing out military leadership and replacing it with people who are loyal—or at least won't say no. He's talked about using the military to shoot protestors, in the past, in 2020. He's talked openly in the past about admiring how China handled Tiananmen Square. We're heading for something ugly and brutal."

Ugly and brutal…and quick. Trump has talked about installing himself as dictator on Day One, and when given the opportunity to walk those comments back, by Sean Hannity and others, doubled down. These intentions cannot be laughed off, or brushed aside as "Trump being Trump." "Being Trump," at this point, is perilously close to being Hitler.

"I know I sound crazy," Tannehill tells me, "but this is—we've seen this historically. They've declared their intention to do this. We see them lining up to do all of this. We see them saying they're going to do this. It's—this is just taking the next step and saying, okay, if they do the thing that they say they're going to do, what is going to be the response."

She is not making this up to scare everybody. They've said, repeatedly, that this is what they plan to do.

The best case scenario is the chaos and financial upheaval that comes with the dismantling of the federal government—which Trump has promised to do, by immediately firing 50,000 federal employees and eliminating certain key departments. Regulations will be a joke, leading to poisoned food, bad medicine, crumbling infrastructure, and so forth. There will be more tax cuts, more income inequality. NATO will fall apart. Putin will win in Ukraine. And if you don't like what Netanyahu is doing to the Palestinians right now, wait until you see how he behaves when given the green light by a president who cares more about building Trump Tower Gaza City than reining in Bibi's more extreme impulses.

That's the best case scenario. The worst case scenario is, the constitutional crises brought on by Red States enforcing antiabortion laws that compel them to arrest people in Blue States for performing medical care, and Blue States resisting—Albany telling Austin to pound sand—are so great, and SCOTUS so impotent and corrupt, that the Union fractures completely, as empires historically do. That would be cataclysmic, and would end badly for Blue and Red States both.

"Trump will use anything within his power, including breaking the system and corrupting the system, to move stuff through. This is an *existential threat* to democracy in America the likes of which we haven't seen since the Civil war," Tannehill says.

"Even more so, perhaps."

I realize that for many readers, and most people generally, this is speculative, pie-in-the-sky stuff: words on a page with no grounding in real life. So, on a recent podcast, I asked Robbie Harris, who in her work with the State Department and USAID has traveled extensively to war-torn countries like Iraq and Syria, what the day-to-day ramifications would be of a second Civil War in the United States.

"Kiss March Madness and the Super Bowl goodbye," she says. "Those things don't happen in the middle of a Civil War. Your Starbucks is gone, and your Walmart is gone, and your gas under $5 a gallon is gone. People are glibly throwing [the idea of Civil War] around, and I hear it from both sides, right? 'Well, maybe we should.' And I'm like, 'You don't know what that means and you don't really mean it.'"

Dismantling the federal government, installing loyalists in positions of power, establishing a system where access to Trump is the most important currency: all of that would breed an instability we haven't seen in this country since the heyday of the original Ku Klux Klan in the post-Reconstruction South—if ever.

In practical terms, living under that kind of corrupt government would objectively suck. It would, Harris says, "affect your daily life, your ability to walk outside of your house, get in your car, drive down the street and pick up your McDonald's, your Chick-fil-A, your Starbucks, whatever it is you want in the morning, with nobody harassing you. Not having to go through armed checkpoints, not having to pay off someone at a checkpoint, not wondering if they're going to shoot your daughter, your son, and knowing that you will get there and be able to purchase what you want and come home safely." This isn't something she's inventing out of whole cloth. This is how daily life *is* in places like Iraq and Syria and Somalia.

To re-state the obvious: fascism blows.

The way to stave off this boot-stomping-on-a-human-face-forever future is to re-elect Joe Biden. Our honorable 81-year-old president is, quite literally, all that stands between us and American tyranny.

But to some people, that's not a bad thing. Incredibly, there *are* Americans—more than you think—who *want* a dictatorship.

VI

RED CAESAR & THE CATHEDRAL
Welcome to the Dark Enlightenment

The Argument: There is an intellectual underpinning to "anti-woke," and it's all about monarchy.

"WOKE" HAS BECOME a rightwing watchword. First used as an adjective by the blues musician Lead Belly, the word was lifted from African-American Vernacular English by well-meaning white leftists and almost immediately appropriated by conservatives, who use it as an umbrella term for all the progressive, do-gooder, social justice-y things they despise.

For Republican politicians, "woke" has been a particularly useful coinage, because, among other things, it serves as a stand-in for "Black," and running on racist dog whistles is a time-honored and effective GOP electoral strategy. But the term does not confine itself to racial justice. "Woke" is expansive, and includes feminism, gay rights, trans rights, animal rights, environmental-ism—whatever liberal *cause célèbre* the stereotypical curmudgeonly uncle might deride during an awkward Thanksgiving dinner-table discussion.

When Ron DeSantis promises that "Florida is where 'woke' goes to die," when Nikki Haley declares that "wokeness is a virus more dangerous than any pandemic," when Elon Musk denounces the "woke mind virus," when the Federalist Society's Leonard Leo decries "the woke idols of our age," they are sending a mes-sage that registers with their acolytes, even as the rest of us—myself very much included—misconstrue the underlying meaning.

For a long time, this overreliance on the word "woke"—little more than a monosyllabic soundbite, overused to the point of parody—struck me as both lazy and dumb. This was red meat for the MAGA base, I figured, which made sense because that audience is also lazy and dumb.

But I underestimated the "anti-woke" movement. There *is* an intellectual underpinning to it. Its tenets *do* cohere, even if its adherents arrive at it from different entryways. It is nihilistic but purposeful, antidemo-cratic if not un-American, seductive, subversive, and at times extremely persuasive—and it has been with us for decades.

ONE OF THE SEMINAL WORKS of "anti-woke" literature, *Industrial Society and Its Future,* was published in 1995 as a supplement to the *Washington Post*. If the title is dull, the manuscript makes for fascinating, if disturbing, reading. The 35,000-word polemic is an overt call for "revolution against the industrial system."

Here is an excerpt from its first section, "The Psychology of Modern Wokeism":

> Almost everyone will agree that we live in a deeply troubled society. One of the most widespread manifestations of the craziness of our world is wokeism, so a discussion of the psychology of wokeism can serve as an introduction to the discussion of the problems of modern society in general.

> But what is wokeism? During the first half of the 20th century wokeism could have been practically identified with socialism. Today the movement is fragmented and it is not clear who can properly be called "woke." When we speak of "woke" in this article we have in mind mainly socialists, collectivists, "politically correct" types, feminists, gay and disability activists, animal rights activists and the like. . . .

> "Wokes" tend to hate anything that has an image of being strong, good and successful. They hate America, they hate Western civilization, they hate white males, they hate rationality. The reasons that woke give for hating the West, etc. clearly do not correspond with their real motives. They SAY they hate the West because it is warlike, imperialistic, sexist, ethnocentric and so forth, but where these same faults appear in socialist countries or in primitive cultures, the woke man finds excuses for them, or at best he GRUDGINGLY admits that they exist; whereas he ENTHUSIASTICALLY points out (and often greatly exaggerates) these

faults where they appear in Western civilization. Thus it is clear that these faults are not the woke man's real motive for hating America and the West. He hates America and the West because they are strong and successful.

Words like "self-confidence," "self-reliance," "initiative," "enterprise," "optimism," etc., play little role in the woke vocabulary. The woke man is anti-individualistic, pro-collectivist. He wants society to solve everyone's problems for them, satisfy everyone's needs for them, take care of them. He is not the sort of person who has an inner sense of confidence in his ability to solve his own problems and satisfy his own needs. The woke man is antagonistic to the concept of competition because, deep inside, he feels like a loser.

And from its penultimate section, "The Danger of Wokeism," we have this:

Our discussion of wokeism has a serious weakness. It is still far from clear what we mean by the word "woke." There doesn't seem to be much we can do about this. Today wokeism is fragmented into a whole spectrum of activist movements. Yet not all activist movements are woke, and some activist movements (e.g., radical environmentalism) seem to include both personalities of the woke type and personalities of thoroughly un-woke types who ought to know better than to collaborate with woke individuals. . . .

The woke man is oriented toward large-scale collectivism. He emphasizes the duty of the individual to serve society and the duty of society to take care of the individual. He has a negative attitude toward individualism. He often takes a moralistic tone. He tends to be for gun control, for sex education and other psychologically "enlightened" educational methods, for social planning, for affirmative action, for multiculturalism. He tends to identify with victims. He tends to be against competition and against violence, but he often finds excuses for those wokes who do commit violence. He is fond of using the common woke catch-phrases, like "racism," "sexism," "homophobia," "capitalism," "imperialism," "neocolonialism," "genocide," "social change," "social justice," "social responsibility." Maybe the best diagnostic trait of the woke man is his tendency to sympathize with the following movements: feminism, gay rights, ethnic rights, disability rights, animal rights, political correctness. Anyone who strongly sympathizes with ALL of these movements is almost certainly woke.

In the great many pages between these two passages, there is much more in this vein.

TL; DR: The country is in trouble because individualistic values are not as highly regarded as they were back in the day. All this tree-hugging and social justice warrioring has made us effete, and since technology only accelerates our decline into fatal effeteness, we must make war on technology. Ned Ludd FTW!

These are unorthodox ideas, to be sure—but then, despite his fancy Harvard education, the author of *Industrial Society and Its Future* was an unorthodox guy. He died last year at FMC Butner, a federal correctional medical facility in North Carolina. His name is Ted Kaczynski. We know him as the Unabomber.

The neo-reactionaries (NRx, for short) refer to him as "Uncle Ted." To understand the tenets, such as they are, of the anti-woke movement, we have to understand Kaczynski's manifesto.

Oh, and if you're wondering how the Unabomber was using the word "woke" in 1995—*mea culpa*, I cheated a little to make my point. In the above excerpts, I swapped out the word "leftist," which is what appears in the original text, for various iterations of "woke." But make no mistake: "woke," in the current sense of the word, is *exactly* what Uncle Ted had in mind.

CURTIS YARVIN IS ARGUABLY the most influential NRx thought leader— "the alt-right's favorite philosophy instructor," as a BBC journalist once called him. The grandson of Jewish American Communists, the son of a U.S. diplomat, and himself (like Kaczynski) a math prodigy, Yarvin graduated from Brown University in 1992—just two semesters after most kids his year, myself included, graduated from high school—and was at UC Berkeley when he dropped out to work as a programmer.

With funding from Peter Thiel—the Frankfurt-born tech billionaire who hovers Sauron-like over the Dark Enlightenment universe—Yarvin formed his own start-up, Tlön Corp, to expand upon Urbit, the decentralized computer network system of his invention.[21]

From 2007-2013, Yarvin wrote rightwing political commentary at Blogger, under the (rather unappealing) pseudonym "Mencius Moldbug." He now produces a Substack called *Gray Mirror.* The New Right magazine

---

[21]   To my tech-ignorant ears, Urbit sounds a lot like Pied Piper from HBO's *Silicon Valley*, and Yarvin bears enough resemblance to Martin Starr's inspired character on the show, Guilfoyle, to make me wonder if he was one of its inspirations.

IM-1776 describes him as a "self-described 'monar-chist'…often credited as the founder of 'neoreaction'" who has "long been one of the leading writers and intellectual figures on the dissident Right." He's a good writer: well-read, persuasive, and often funny. As an intellectual exercise, I enjoyed engaging with his ideas, as off-putting as I often found them, because they made me question my own. I get why he is held in high regard by the neo-reactionary fringe.

One of NRx's foundational concepts is "the Cathedral," a term Yarvin coined "a *long* long time ago" and about which he harbors "ambivalent aesthetic feelings." (Me, I like it.) Rather than put words in his mouth, I'll let him describe the concept himself:

> "The cathedral" is just a short way to say "journalism plus academia"—in other words, the intellectual institutions at the center of modern society, just as the Church was the intellectual institution at the center of medieval society.

> But the label is making a point. The Catholic Church is *one* institution—the cathedral is *many* institutions. Yet the label is singular. This trans-formation from many to one—literally, *e pluribus unum*—is the heart of the mystery at the heart of the modern world.

> The mystery of the cathedral is that all the mod-ern world's legitimate and prestigious intellectual institutions, even though they have no central organizational connection, behave in many ways as if they were a *single* organizational structure.

Most notably, this pseudo-structure is *synoptic*: it has one clear doctrine or perspective. *It always agrees with itself.* Still more puzzlingly, its doctrine is not static; it evolves; this doctrine has a predictable direction of evolution, and the *whole structure moves together.*

and

The professors and journalists have sovereignty because final decisions are entrusted to them and there is no power above them. Only professors can formulate policy—that is, set government strategy; only journalists can hold government accountable—that is, manage government tactics. Strategy plus tactics equals control.

Having dabbled in both academia and journalism, I can say with some assurance that, while both undoubtedly have influence over key decisions—especially collectively, in the way Yarvin is talking about—neither professors nor journalists are the final arbiters of *anything.* Nevertheless, I think I understand what he means.

In 1922, Walter Lippman, in his groundbreaking book *Public Opinion*, suggested that intellectuals and experts in various fields—collectively, "a specialized class whose interests reach beyond the locality"—are necessary for democracies to function, as the "bewildered herd" of popular voters cannot be relied upon to know anything about anything, much less everything about everything. A hundred years later, that specialized class has prevailed, and expanded, and, per Yarvin (and per Lippmann), accrued power. The Cathedral, as I understand it, is Mencius Moldbug's poetical name for Lippmann's class of experts.

Another New Right thought leader, former private equity guy and Trump's Deputy Assistant to the President for Strategic Communications Michael Anton, also recognizes and despises the Cathedral, which in his view isn't limited to academics and reporters. "[T]he people we nominally elect don't hold real power," he writes in an essay for *Up from Conservatism: Revitalizing the Right after a Generation of Decay*, a new anthology edited by the head of the Claremont Institute's Center for the American Way of Life. "And when they do, they often use it for unconstitutional ends. America's real rulers are not the constitutional officers we vote for, and certainly not the American people, whom our understanding of political legitimacy asserts to be sovereign. They are, rather, a network of unelected bureaucrats, revolving-door cabinet and subcabinet officials, corporate-tech-finance senior management, 'experts' who set the boundaries of acceptable opinion, and media figures who police those boundaries."

The Hillsdale College professor Kevin Slack expands the Cathedral even wider. In an influential *cris de coeur* with the Orwellian title *War on the American Republic: How Liberalism Became Despotism*, Slack rails against an "entire cosmopolitan class that includes much of the entrenched bureaucracy, the military, the media, and government-sponsored corporations." That's a fancy way of saying "The Deep State."

Lippmann holds that the Cathedral is necessary for a democracy to properly function; Yarvin, Anton, Slack, and their fellow neo-reactionaries want it eradicated. As best as I can tell, Trump's ominous campaign promise to immediately fire a vast segment of the civil service has its roots in an acronym Yarvin made up: RAGE, or Retire All Government Employees.

This notion of a specialized class is not a particularly controversial idea. They are not wrong. In the aggregate, the Cathedral—or whatever name you wish to assign to it—really *does* hold enormous power over governmental policy, artistic taste, societal mores, public opinion, and so forth. And the NRx guys should know, as all three of them are members in good standing of the very "cosmopolitan class" they revile: Slack is a college professor; Anton, a revolving-door official and corporate-tech-finance executive; and Yarvin, an influential member of the media (if not, to be accurate, what he calls "the *legitimate* press.")

So the million-dollar question is not *whether* the Cathedral exists, but whether it *should*.

ONE OF THE MAIN DRAWBACKS of the U.S. government is that, because power is diffuse, change cannot happen quickly. This is by design—the checks and balances we learned about in elementary school. The two chambers of Congress seldom march in lockstep. The President has veto power over bills sent to his desk. The Supreme Court can toss out, on a whim, any law it doesn't like. The last time that Capitol Hill got legislation passed lickety-split was during FDR's Hundred Days. Roosevelt was creative, fast, and efficient; he threw a shit-ton of legislative spaghetti at the wall; he had healthy majorities in both House and Senate—and even *then*, the Supreme Court shot down some of his more grandiose agenda items.

A small-r republican system of government does not lend itself well to fast, radical change; a democracy, even less so. What does is a dictatorship. And when the changes you want to make are deeply unpopular with the voting public—think eradication of abortion, privatization of Social Security, elimination of gay rights, or total deregulation of firearms—the surest way to ensure their implementation is if a dictator—a "Red Caesar"—imposes them on an unwilling citizenry. Therein lies the appeal of autocracy to the NRx set.

As Slack, the Hillsdale professor, writes:

> Small republican communities may have little power against an insulated national bureaucracy, but perhaps the New Right's own cultural revolution is the fertile soil for political revolution, either as autonomous islands of republican civilization in an increasingly fragmenting order or the bulwark for a Caesar. At some point in the decline of every empire, with its dissolute senators, it finally dawns on a truly great leader, one born of the family of the lion or the tribe of the eagle, "Hey, I could run this thing." The New Right now often discusses a Red Caesar, by which is meant a leader whose post-Constitutional rule will restore the strength of his people.

Yarvin sees our existing government as "a *bureaucracy*, which is one kind of *oligarchy*. ('Deep State,' if you absolutely *must*.)" He argues that the Cathedral is beyond repair—and he may well be right on that point—because power leaks all over the place. But his solution is extreme: "An organization which focuses responsibility toward the top, without leaking, is an organization structured like an army or a corporation. In this form of organization (used by almost everything that isn't a government), your manager actually *is* your boss. Final authority and responsibility lands on one person," he writes. "This form of government—the form that doesn't leak power—has a name. It is called a *monarchy*."

As Americans, our first instinct is to reject monarchy wholesale, just as the Founding Fathers did 250 years ago. Didn't the Sons of Liberty skunk an entire shipload of tea to thwart a king? Wasn't there, in recent memory, a rightwing political movement *called* the Tea Party? Why should we even consider such a drastic step?

Monarchy does have certain advantages. In the interview with IM-1776, Yarvin cites the work of the UNLV professor emeritus Hans-Hermann Hoppe (another Cathedral member!), the author of *Democracy: The God That Failed* and a vociferous opponent of democracy. "Hoppe [points out] that a hereditary monarchy in the classic European style, far from being a barbaric relic, is simply a [sovereign corporation] that's a family business," Yarvin explains. "Because the time horizon of a family is indefinite, like the time horizon of a state, the hereditary monarch exhibits the least tension between personal and national interests."

Well, sure, but that doesn't mean living under a monarchy—or, more likely, a soft dictatorship—would be a walk in the park, for the poor *or* for the rich. Traditionally, kings have a way of extracting tribute from their wealthy subjects in amounts that would give Grover Norquist the vapors. There's a reason why Thomas Jefferson *et alii* ixnayed George III.

For the rest of us, meanwhile, autocracy seems antithetical to liberty—although Kaczynski didn't think so. Uncle Ted points out that "[m]ost of the Indian nations of New England were monarchies, and many of the cities of the Italian Renaissance were controlled by dictators. But in reading about these societies one gets the impression that they allowed far more personal freedom than our society does." Nice that the Unabomber formed that impression from books, but survivors of the despotic Soviet bloc regimes—and most Iranians today—would respectfully disagree.

The thing is, a King of America *would* tear down the Cathedral—an end that would, in the NRx view, justify the means. "An absolute hereditary monarch has no interest in employing a dysfunctional bureaucracy," Yarvin says. "Since he wants to see his nation thrive, he is more likely to adopt the economic and social system that seems to make nations thrive: libertarian capitalism. So we come full circle, in a kind of layer-cake of libertarianism, then absolute monarchy, then more libertarianism."

Here, Yarvin is operating under a false assumption. The historical evidence is overwhelming that absolute monarchs are less interested in seeing their *nations* thrive than in seeing *themselves* thrive—whether through bloody conquest, amassment of riches, or decadent hedonism. The annals of imperial Rome are littered with self-absorbed, feckless, ineffectual emperors. For every Marcus Aurelius there are dozens of Elagabaluses. Yes, there have been exceptional kings, emperors, sultans. But they are just that—exceptions. Most are at best ho-hum, and if their nations prosper, it is in spite of them and not because of them. The Roman Empire, the Byzantine Empire, and the British Empire owed their longevity to robust bureaucratic systems that were durable enough to withstand the meddling of useless monarchs—the Roman, Byzantine, and British equivalents of the Cathedral.

Then there is the matter of *how* the United States might acquire a hereditary king: by coup d'état. A president would have to seize power, crumple up the Constitution, dismantle the apparatus of government, and declare himself Ruler for Life. Joe Biden is not going to do this, just as George Washington didn't, or the Roosevelts, or Eisenhower, or Reagan. The only guy who *would* do such a thing is the presumptive Republican 2024 presidential nominee, Donald John Trump. Which means we wouldn't get the family of the lion or the tribe of the eagle; we'd get the ass of the horse.

As unlikely as all of this sounds, the threat is real. As the *Philadelphia Inquirer*'s Will Bunch—to my knowledge the first columnist from a major U.S. newspaper to take this seriously—wrote in a column earlier last October, when "a desire to blow it all up" is "translated by the extreme right's 'intellectuals' into an explicit plea for a dictatorship, you can see that America is poised to cross the Rubicon—a metaphor rooted in the river in northern Italy that Julius Caesar had to cross with his army in 49 B.C. in order to drive out Rome's democratically elected government and seize power." Heck, "Rubicon" even *sounds* like a convention of New Right dissidents.

Unpopularity alone is not enough to prevent the current Bedford Falls incarnation of the United States from morphing into a Pottersville of Kevin Slack's wildest dreams. As Uncle Ted points out, "[R]evolutionaries should not expect to have a majority of people on their side. History is made by active, determined minorities, not by the majority, which seldom has a clear and consistent idea of what it really wants."

My guess is, a return to monarchy is one of those "seldom" occasions when the will of the majority would be pretty clear and consistent. But even if the majority of Americans somehow *wanted* an absolute monarch, why on earth would we opt for King Donald I?

The more urgent question is: why do *they* want that?

ON THE STUMP, railing against "woke" comes off as pandering. "Florida is where 'woke' goes to die" would sound bad-ass if Clint Eastwood were muttering it in a *Dirty Harry* picture, but when given voice by Ron DeSantis, whom no one ever confused with Clint Eastwood, the phrase sounds both hollow and ridiculous—not least because what actually goes to Florida to die is not "woke," but rather a healthy percentage of his constituency, who may not wish to be reminded of this actuarial fact.

Seriously, though: what does that even mean? Who are the "woke" that are being threatened with their lives in the Sunshine State? The answer: trans people, gays and lesbians, women who want or need abortions, people of color, liberal college professors, elementary school teachers, doctors, journalists who ask hard questions. I'm no James Carville or Steve Schmidt, but issuing a sort of papal bull condemning to death a significant swath of the voting public seems like maybe not the most prudent political strategy.

And yet almost all the Republican politicians do it—even the presumed normies like Nikki Haley. Either they've all come down with the anti-woke mind virus, or the word is valuable currency in that post-truth realm—enough to make it worth the risk of alienating a sizable chunk of registered voters.

Even Leonard Leo—rightwing SCOTUS whisperer, co-founder of the Federalist Society, reactionary legal activist, Knight of Malta, and beneficiary of $1.6 billion to put to work on his radical Catholic agenda (more on this extremely powerful weirdo in the next chapter)—has adopted the buzzword. In a video promoting one of his many projects, the Teneo Network, an outfit *Pro Publica* describes as a "Federalist Society for everything," Leo says: "I spent close to 30 years, if not more, helping to build the conservative legal movement. And at some point or another, I just said to myself, 'If this can work for law, why can't it work for lots of other areas of American culture and American life where things are really messed up right now?'" He goes on to explain that these problems in American life and culture involve "wokeism in the corporate environment [and] in the educational environment."

"The idea behind the network and the enterprise we built is to roll back liberal dominance in many important sectors of American life," Leo continued. "I had a couple of decades or more of experience rolling back liberal dominance in the legal culture, and I thought it was time to take the lessons learned from that and see whether there was a way to roll back liberal dominance in other areas of American cultural, policy, and political life."

But how do they plan to decontaminate corporate America and the U.S. public education system of virulent wokeness? Is it even *possible*, in the Year of Our Lord 2024, to roll back liberal dominance in cultural, policy, and political life?

Back in 2013, at a book party at his D.C. townhouse, Steven K. Bannon explained his political philosophy to the author Ron Radosh: "I'm a Leninist," he said. "Lenin wanted to destroy the state, and that's my goal too. I want to bring everything crashing down, and destroy all of today's establishment."

Time did not mellow him. Bannon went on to become Trump's campaign chairman and then his White House chief strategist. His mission, he said in 2017, was nothing less than the "deconstruction of the administrative state."

This was not just bluster. At the time, you might recall, Trump was busy lining his Cabinet with loyalists who hated the existence of the departments they were tasked to head, or else were too inept to do the job properly. Betsy DeVos as Secretary of Education? Rex Tillerson, the former head of Exxon, at State? A climate change denier at the EPA? John Ratcliffe and Ric Grenell as DNI?

Fortunately, our institutions were strong enough to withstand their incompetent leadership. When the buildings are made of stone, there's only so much damage an arsonist can do.

That won't be the case in a Trump sequel. The moderating forces have been purged. Trump will appoint loyalists, lackeys, and Leninists, in the Bannon sense of the term, to positions of power. The result will be devastating. First to go: the civil service. Trump will take to heart Curtis Yarvin's "RAGE" directive: Retire All Government Employees.

As Eric Katz explains in *Government Executive*, Trump's plan

> would bring back Schedule F, a workforce initiative Trump pushed in the 11th hour of his term to politicize the federal bureaucracy. The former officials and current confidantes are, through a network of Trump-loyal think tanks and public policy organizations, creating lists of names to supplant existing civil servants. They have identified 50,000 current employees that could be dismissed under the new authority they seek to create, *Axios* reported and *Government Executive* confirmed, though they hope to only actually fire a fraction of that total and hope the resulting "chilling effect" will cause the rest to fall in line.

Trump won't stop there. Aid to Ukraine will end. So will funding for Jack Smith's investigations. He will weaponize the Justice Department, ordering whatever monster he installs as Attorney General to immediately end the cases against him and instead go after his political rivals. Journalists will be under attack, and scientists, and college professors—Yarvin's "Cathedral," Bannon's "establishment," Anton's "regime." The criminalization of abortion will expand. He may well order a compliant Congress to expand the Supreme Court, and let Leonard Leo pick the newcomers. And he will pardon himself, his family, and every last J6 plotter, forming a private army of faithful mercenaries.

Is this really the future the NRx desires? Why would anyone not named Jared or Ivanka want that?

Destruction, remember, is revolution. As Ted Kaczynski correctly observes in his manifesto:

> It will be objected that the French and Russian Revolutions were failures. But most revolutions have two goals. One is to destroy an old form of society and the other is to set up the new form of society envisioned by the revolutionaries. The French and Russian revolutionaries failed (fortunately!) to create the new kind of society of which they dreamed, but they were quite successful in destroying the old society.

Maybe the United States turns into a fascist dictatorship. Maybe Leonard Leo coronates King Donald I at the National Cathedral. Maybe another pandemic, caused by climate change, sweeps through the country, killing off a third the population, and there are no scientists left to make new vaccines. Maybe the Northeast states and the Pacific Coast states secede from the Union, on the grounds that the Constitution does not demand allegiance to a monarch. Maybe there will be an actual second Civil War, like the MAGA trolls have been calling for for years.

The New Right doesn't care. They don't care. To the neo-reactionaries, *any* outcome is preferable to the woke society we live in now. As long as the Cathedral—or the Deep State, or the regime, or whatever you want to call it—comes tumbling down, it's all good, as far as they're concerned. They don't care. Let me reiterate: They. Don't. Care.

The Unabomber—"Uncle Ted," to them—expresses the objective unambiguously: "We have no illusions about the feasibility of creating a new, ideal form of society," he writes. "Our goal is only to destroy the existing form of society."

VII
DICTATORSHIP FOR DUMMIES
Project 2025's counter-reformation

The Argument: Plans are in place to topple democracy and bring about an American dictatorship.

OCCUPYING THE CENTER of an intricate web of political, legal, religious, and business connections, Leonard Leo is the quintessential Man in the Middle, a veritable dark-money spider. Like a spider, he is patient, painstaking, relentless, and much more powerful than he appears. And like a spider, he prefers to stay hidden. To wit: I've mentioned him a few times already in this book, and you probably didn't even notice. But who is this mystery man Clarence Thomas once called the third most powerful individual in the country?

What Leonard Leo wants you to know about Leonard Leo, insofar as he wants you to know anything at all, is that, first and foremost, he is a Knight of Malta. The Sovereign Military Order of Malta (SMOM) is a lay Catholic order that claims descent from the Knights Hospitaller, founded in Jerusalem in 1099, at the end of the First Crusade. It's an extremely selective group. Of the 1.2 billion Catholics in the world, only 13,000 are Knights of Malta—although most of them don't go around bragging about it.

Leo, I'm told, is very proud of this honor. First, because it demonstrates just how radically Catholic his radical Catholicism runs. And second, because it speaks to his importance. SMOM membership is the sort of status symbol that eluded him, growing up middle-class in the suburbs of New Jersey, where his Monroe Township High School classmates derisively nicknamed him "Moneybags." His mother and step-father weren't blue bloods. He wasn't some wealthy boarding school kid. Poor guy had to make due with *Cornell* instead of Harvard or Yale. He was a nobody.

But look at him now! Leonard Leo, who turns 60 next year, has made himself one of the most powerful figures in the United States. He's put five—count 'em, *five!*—justices on the Supreme Court: Amy Coney Barrett, Brett Kavanaugh, Neil Gorsuch, Sam Alito, and John Roberts. A sixth, Clarence Thomas, is one of his closest friends. And, perhaps most impressively, he quietly led the 2016 crusade to deny Merrick Garland a hearing, when Barack Obama nominated the centrist jurist to replace the late Antonin Scalia (another of Leo's pals). In the lower courts, he's been even busier. He's installed so many judges on so many courts, it makes you wonder if he really *is* the instrument of God's will he believes himself to be. I mean, there are only three branches of government. One of those three—arguably the most important one—is Leonard Leo's domain.

You wouldn't know it to look at him. Leonard Leo is a short, foppish, pear-shaped man, in wire-rimmed glasses and pricey suits. Think a dandier George Constanza, or if The Penguin worked at Jones Day. As Jeffrey Toobin wrote in the 2017 *New Yorker* profile (that is now framed in Leo's office):

> Leo is at ease in the role of impresario. His grandfather was a vice-president of Brooks Brothers, and he instilled in young Leonard a taste for the *bella figura*. Leo wears tailored suits, often with contrasting waistcoats, and a double-length gold fob attached to a 1935 train conductor's pocket watch. ("The most accurate watch in the United States until the fifties," he said.) In lieu of office meetings, Leo prefers to chat over breakfast (just bacon, no eggs) at the Hay-Adams Hotel, across from the White House. As his friend Boyden Gray, the White House counsel under George H. W. Bush, puts it, "He knows the best restaurants in every major city in the world, and the best wines. He has a wide-ranging, inquiring mind, and he can and will talk about any subject under the sun."

When I first began researching Leonard Leo in 2021, I didn't know much about the guy beyond his silly, comic-book-villain name. I was surprised to discover that he was, like me, a middle-class product of Catholic upbringing and Italian descent who graduated from a public high school in New Jersey—not at all the well-heeled, oenophilic Master of the Universe he has become. He's also much younger than I expected; born in 1965, he's solidly Gen X.

Yet Leonard Leo, somehow, is the individual most responsible for stripping away federal abortion rights. As his admiring chum Ed Wheelan presciently wrote in 2016, "No one has been more dedicated to the enterprise of building a Supreme Court that will overturn *Roe v. Wade* than the Federalist Society's Leonard Leo."

Leo's is a dour, zero-sum faith—pure, inflexible, unswerving. Less inquisition, more Inquisition. He believes absolutely in the Holy Trinity of fundamentalist Catholic political dogma: no birth control, no LGBTQ rights, no abortions. And this is no act. When I asked if Leo's religious beliefs were sincere, Tom Carter, who was communications director at USCIRF from 2009-2012, when Leo was the *de facto* chief, told me: "He believes he's on a mission from God." That monomaniacal mission is to mold the judicial branch to his liking, and in so doing, to do away with *Roe* (check), protections for the LGBTQ community (coming in a second Trump term), and contraception (ditto).

To give you a taste of Leo's vibe, here are some remarks he made at an address at Benedictine College last year: "The barbarians are determined to threaten and delegitimize individuals and institutions who refuse to pledge fealty to the woke idols of our age. The secularists are fine with Catholics in the public square so long as we don't, you know, practice our faith. They want us to draw the curtains at home and keep it in the pews, and it remains to be seen how long they'll accept even that."

Those critical of his despotic, reactionary predilections—you know, us barbarians—Leo dismissed as "progressive bigots" who "distort who we are and what we believe in, and will go so far as to intimidate or harass us in public in an effort to drive us into professional and social exile." In addition to other rights he wants to take away, then, we can add freedom of assembly and freedom of speech.

To be clear, there are plenty of American Catholics who are pro-choice and pro-LGBTQ rights. President Biden, to name one. Justice Sonia Sotomayor, to name another. I was raised Catholic and am now what you'd call a cultural Catholic. But Leo doesn't just want any old Catholic on the high court. If so, he would have been jumping for joy about Sotomayor's selection. He wants *radical* Catholics.

Along with former Attorney General Bill Barr, Leonard Leo served on the board of the Catholic Information Center, the Opus Dei stronghold on K Street in Washington, a few blocks from the White House. As such, he must have been influenced by the former head of that same Catholic Information Center, Father C. John McCloskey, an Opus Dei priest. McCloskey was singlehandedly responsible for recruiting a number of powerful Washington insiders to… well, if not Opus Dei proper, then something decidedly un-American. This is from a piece Charles P. Pierce wrote for the *Boston Globe* in 2003, about a group he termed "The Crusaders":

> There is a glow to the priest when he talks…He is talking about a futuristic essay he wrote that rosily describes the aftermath of a "relatively bloodless" civil war that resulted in a Catholic Church purified of all dissent and the religious dismemberment of the United States of America.
>
> "There's two questions there," says the Rev. C. John McCloskey 3d, smiling…"One is, Do I think it would be better that way? No. Do I think it's

possible? Do I think it's possible for someone who believes in the sanctity of marriage, the sanctity of life, the sanctity of family, over a period of time to choose to survive with people who think it's OK to kill women and children or for—quote—homosexual couples to exist and be recognized?

"No, I don't think that's possible," he says. "I don't know how it's going to work itself out, but I know it's not possible, and my hope and prayer is that it does not end in violence. But, unfortunately, in the past, these types of things have tended to end this way.

"If American Catholics feel that's troubling, let them. I don't feel it's troubling at all."

McCloskey spoke of a "relatively bloodless" civil war, because it's "not possible" for people like him to peacefully coexist with the LGBTQ community. Barr seeks a "traditional moral order." Leo, as Jay Michaelson succinctly explains in *The Daily Beast*, believes that "most of the New Deal and administrative state are unconstitutional, that corporations have free speech and free religion rights, that women and LGBT people are not 'protected classes' under constitutional law, and that there is no right to privacy implied by the due process clause of the Constitution (i.e., banning abortion, contraception, and gay marriage are entirely constitutional)."

The thing is, those are unpopular positions, reviled by a healthy majority of Americans. Given the demographic trends in the United States, the only way "The Crusaders" can bring the country back to the pre-New Deal era is to establish a dictatorship—a radical Catholic caliphate. Leonard Leo and his buddies are clearly okay with that. The Opus Dei prelature, remember, has its origins in Fascist Spain. The Roman Catholic Church is very much a top-down organization—what the Pope says goes. The late J. Peter Grace, the head of the American Knights of Malta, whose Maine compound Leo now owns, was reportedly involved in Operation Paperclip, and was therefore okay with Nazis. Steve Bannon and the NRx want to destroy the American administrative state—the Cathedral. By eradicating the barrier between Church and State, Leo seeks the same outcome. Ultimately, what these men want is, to put it mildly, inconsistent with democracy. That makes them particularly dangerous. They see Trump in Machiavellian terms: as the means to an end.

But it's not only faith that animates Leonard Leo. As *Politico's* Heidi Przybyla reported last March, Leo has been rewarded handsomely for his troubles. "I personally don't believe that Leonard is motivated by greed," Steven Calabresi, who founded the Federalist Society with Leo and still runs the organization, told Przybyla. "I think Leonard is motivated by ideology and ideas. I do think he likes to live a high-rolling lifestyle, but I don't think he's in the business because of the money."

To be fair, Leo *does* spread that money around. He endows more organizations than I can succinctly list here. Friends like Ginni Thomas—wife of Clarence—get a taste. He brings his SCOTUS cronies on lavish fishing trips with his billionaire backers, as *ProPublica* reported. And yet Leo has amassed a fortune for himself, and spends that fortune lavishly: on tailored suits, palatial vacation homes in Maine, and bottles of wine that cost more than what most Americans pay for a month's rent.

So how does he do it? How does he wield so much power? Networking. Like an invasive cancer, Leonard

Leo has metastasized from the Federalist Society to the broader conservative legal community. He knows anyone and everyone, from John Roberts to Mick Mulvaney to Ed Whelan to Kellyanne Conway to the sommelier at Morton's who pours out the vino. Despite being a generation younger, he was good friends with the late Antonin Scalia and remains tight with Clarence Thomas. He delights in pulling the marionette strings. "He likes to place people," Carter told me.

But it's the *financial* networking that moves the needle. Leo sits like a giant spider at the center of a complicated web of non-profits and PACs and 501-whatevers: The Federalist Society, which identifies, develops, and grooms future conservative judges. The Judicial Crisis Network, the PR arm of the operation. The Becket Fund, a legal outfit that does pro bono work for religious freedom cases. The Freedom and Opportunity Fund, which helped bankroll the Brett Kavanaugh nomination hoo-ha. Reclaim New York, a charity Leo set up in 2013 with Rebekah Mercer and Steve Bannon. The Council for National Policy, the Christian coalition group. And God knows how many others.

For non-profits, these entities sure do rake in the cash. Leo's association with Mercer and Bannon, for example, was a veritable gold mine. As the *Washington Post* reported in 2019:

> Between 2014 and 2017 alone, they collected more than $250 million in such donations, sometimes known as "dark money," according to a Post analysis of the most recent tax filings available. The money was used in part to support conservative policies and judges, through advertising and through

funding for groups whose executives appeared as
television pundits.

The groups in Leo's network often work in concert
and are linked to Leo and one another by finances,
shared board members, phone numbers, addresses,
back-office support and other operational details,
according to tax filings, incorporation records,
other documents and interviews.

That's a *quarter of a billion dollars* in dark money
donations. And more than a little of that dark money
wound up in his pocket. At the time of the Brett
Kavanaugh nomination process, Leonard Leo reportedly
paid off the mortgage on his own home in McLean,
Virginia, and also scooped up a $3.3 million luxury
estate on the Maine coast. He paid almost a million
bucks less than the appraised value of the home, which
was sold to him by Grace, a fellow Knight of Malta,
as mentioned.

The rest of that vast pool of dough sloshes around
from one dark money org to the next, where it can best
be deployed. Leo plants op-eds in newspapers, and
he buys ads, and he hires PR outfits to do marketing
campaigns, and he lobbies, and he does it in such a way
that no one can see the radical-Catholic Oz behind the
curtain, with his gold fob and his decanter of Château
Lafite.

And now, thanks to the biggest dark money donation
of all, Leo has virtually unlimited financial resources.
The 91-year-old reclusive billionaire Barre Seid—his
name rhymes with "parricide"—bequeathed $1.6 billion
of his vast fortune to Leo to use as he sees fit. That's
$1.6 billion, with a "b," an almost unfathomable pile of
cash. As Nina Burleigh writes in the *New Republic*, the

$1,600,000,000 gift is basically "altruism in reverse: a fire hose of cash aimed at destroying American liberal culture through lawsuits and support for politicians challenging gay rights, unions, environmental protection, voting rights, and public education."

Barre Seid has passed the one-point-six-billion-dollar baton to Leo, the dark money maestro, who will conduct an aria of his own. And because of the breathtaking size of the endowment, in Leonard Leo's metaphorical opera, the fat lady will never sing. Burleigh explains this horror:

> The money will last a good long while. Philanthropic recipients usually follow a 5 percent rule: They try not to spend more than 5 percent of the endowment per year. Seid's pile is so large that it could return an average $136 million a year, or north of $230 million on a good year, to influence U.S. law and policy. Without ever having to touch the nut. For a sense of how enormous that is, consider this. The Heritage Foundation and its affiliates spent about $86 million in 2021. Heritage is a huge, and hugely influential, conservative think tank. Leo could create two Heritage Foundations and one more sizable organization on the side—all, again, without having to dip into the principal at all.

Another rich soulless libertarian asshole, Elon Musk, won't stop yammering about the "woke mind virus." That's a poor analogy, though. What more closely resembles a virus is the Seid gift to Leo. Once released into the world, that self-perpetuating dark-money fortune is almost impossible to get rid of. It is a herpes sore. It will flare up again and again and again, *ad infinitum,* because there is no easy cure for *Citizens United.* The war chest regenerates like the liver of Prometheus. Seid has gifted Leonard Leo all the Infinity Stones. Spend five percent, invest the rest, and the interest alone will finance far-right activity until Florida sinks into the sea.

Most Americans don't share Leonard Leo's creepy, fascistic predilections. All the money in the world won't make his extreme anti-abortion, anti-woman, virulently homophobic policies popular. But if you essentially purchase the entire judicial branch of the federal government, and you use your considerable influence in the statehouses to gerrymander the hell out of the districts to tilt the vote your way, the will of the people becomes secondary to the will of a radical-Catholic weirdo from Central Jersey with a passion for enjoying fine wine and stripping away the rights of women and the LGBTQ community. As Burleigh puts it—and this is not hyperbole—"Medieval popes had less power."

Popes, of course, like their robed counterparts on the U.S. Supreme Court, get the job for life. Even the corrupt and odious likes of John XII, Alexander VI, and Leo X died eventually. Neither Leonard Leo nor Clarence Thomas nor Sam Alito nor John Roberts are immortal. But Seid's fortune has eternal life.

LIKE MANY LEADERS of the reactionary right—Mike Johnson, Mike Davis, Stephen Miller, and so on—the current head of the Heritage Foundation has a dull, forgettable name: Kevin Roberts. He has a friendly manner, a doctorate in U.S. history, a background in academia, and a well-earned reputation as a nice guy. Who could have imagined that this bright, friendly Gen Xer would be leading a Christian conservative counter-reformation—a crusade to end American democracy?

In 2013, Roberts, who like Leonard Leo is a radical Catholic, became the second president of Wyoming Catholic College, a strict, almost monastic institution established in 2007 that provides, its website says, "a rigorous immersion in the primary sources of the classical liberal arts tradition, the grandeur of the mountain wilderness, and the spiritual heritage of the Catholic Church." When he took the reins, no one had heard of the place. He made national headlines in 2015 by rejecting Title IX federal student loans and grants; Wyoming Catholic refused to follow guidelines imposed by federal bureaucrats. They answered to God, not Washington. An article in the *New York Times* dubbed the maverick new president and his charges "cowboy Catholics," an alliterative bit of branding that Roberts leaned into. Now, graduates of the ascendant college receive a black Stetson cowboy hat with their degree.

From Wyoming, the Cowboy Catholic moved back to Texas, working at the Texas Public Policy Foundation, a think tank best known for promoting climate change denialism. He took the job at Heritage in the fall of 2021. He was not a conventional choice. But a dude media-savvy enough to put tiny Wyoming Catholic on the radar could clearly do much more at an august operation like Heritage.

And so he has. Under his guidance, Roberts organized Project 2025: Presidential Transition Project, a plan for "institutionalizing Trumpism," as he told the *New York Times*. "[T]he Trump administration, with the best of intentions, simply got a slow start," he explained. "And Heritage and our allies in Project 2025 believe that must never be repeated." Those allies, listed in the front of the book, include a healthy chunk of Leonard Leo-affiliated organizations: all that dirty Barre Seid money sloshing around.

The fruit of this Presidential Transition Project labor is the 920-page *Mandate for Leadership: The Conservative Promise*, a sort of Baedeker for how to quickly, neatly, and radically lurch the federal government from republic to Orbán-style Christofascist autocracy. (Roberts, like so many Christian conservatives, loves him some Hungarian "illiberal democracy.") Among its 400 contributors are Trump administration retreads Ezra Cohen-Watnick, Christopher Miller, Ken Cuccinelli, Rick Dearborn, John Ratcliffe, Anthony Tata, and the felon Peter Navarro; Leonard Leo associates Roger Severino and Austin Ruse; and Ginni Thomas bestie and subpoena dodger Cleta Mitchell, best known for being on the phone call when Donald Trump asked Georgia Secretary of State Brad Raffensperger to scrounge up votes.

In the book's foreword, Roberts invokes battlefield terminology, calling the contents of the tome "the opening salvo of the 2025 Presidential Transition Project." He writes, "Its 30 chapters lay out hundreds of clear and concrete policy recommendations for White House offices, Cabinet departments, Congress, and agencies, commissions, and boards." And, in case anyone missed the point, he adds (boldface mine): "This is **an agenda prepared by and for conservatives who will be ready on Day One of the next Administration** to save our country from the brink of disaster."

Make no mistake: if Trump were to be re-elected, he would install *these* loyalists and implement *these* policies. A second incoming Trump administration, unlike the first incoming one, would be immediately purged of anyone who did not put Donald over country. And they'd impose all of this stuff right quick, *Shock Doctrine* style, before we knew what hit us. At least, that's *The Conservative Promise*'s promise.

To get a taste of what this new America might look like, we need only peruse Roberts's foreword to the book, which reads like Margaret Atwood fan fiction. Project 2025 seeks to undo all the progress made in the country since, basically, the McKinley assassination. That's why I call it a "counter-reformation." Heritage is pushing back on 12 decades of popular reforms that have made all of our lives better (including theirs). Roberts & Co. want to mortally wound government regulation, claw back civil rights advancements, eliminate numerous federal agencies, do away with all that woke New Deal stuff, and replace the brain trust at the CDC and the NIH and NASA and DARPA with *[checks notes]* "parents at a high school football game in Waco, Texas."

Roberts *loathes* experts in exactly the way he (wrongly) believes that uppity Leftists loathe him. "Intellectual sophistication, advanced degrees, financial success, and all other markers of elite status have no bearing on a person's knowledge of the one thing most necessary for governance: what it means to live well," he writes. By that metric, the country should be run by the Rich Kids of Instagram. Which, if Trump is re-elected, it kinda sorta will.

THE FOREWORD TO *Mandate for Leadership* is a revealing document. What does the nation's future look like to Kevin Roberts? What are the planks in the Cowboy Catholic's Counter-Reformation? Here are ten take-aways, all of them ominous:

1. Straight married families with children will enjoy favored status.

Front and center is a focus on family. And not just any family—man and wife joined in holy matrimony, and the children born in wedlock to said couple. Other family dynamics are scapegoated and scorned.

Roberts also sets up a Reaganite argument that government is 1) inherently bad, and 2) something other than We The People organized for good governance. To Roberts, *community* is the people; *government* is a just bunch of faceless, power-mad bureaucrats. This excerpt gives some insight into his thinking:

> The next conservative President must get to work pursuing the true priority of politics—the well-being of the American family. In many ways, the entire point of centralizing political power is to subvert the family. Its purpose is to replace people's natural loves and loyalties with unnatural ones. You see this in the popular left-wing aphorism, "Government is simply the name we give to the things we choose to do together." But in real life, most of the things people "do together" have nothing to do with government. These are the mediating institutions that serve as the building blocks of any healthy society. Marriage. Family. Work. Church. School. Volunteering. The name real people give to the things we do together is community, not government. Our lives are full of interwoven, overlapping communities, and our individual and collective happiness depends upon them. But the most important community in each of our lives—and the life of the nation—is the family.

Not that "traditional" families aren't important. I'm the product of one, and I'm a member of one right now. I just don't think they should be treated like the

Brahmins in the American caste system, the paradigm for all that is right and good.

2. Gay, Lesbian, and non-binary individuals will be stripped of their civil rights.

Opposed to the idea of helping the LGBT community on theological grounds, Roberts proposes that we simply *not acknowledge the existence of* what he calls, I think derisively, "SOGI":

> The next conservative President must make the institutions of American civil society hard targets for woke culture warriors. This starts with deleting the terms sexual orientation and gender identity ("SOGI"), diversity, equity, and inclusion ("DEI"), gender, gender equality, gender equity, gender awareness, gender-sensitive, abortion, reproductive health, reproductive rights, and any other term used to deprive Americans of their First Amendment rights out of every federal rule, agency regulation, contract, grant, regulation, and piece of legislation that exists.

Every federal rule? *Every* piece of legislation? That means the end of marriage equality, the end of transitioning, the end of LGBT as a protected class under federal law—protected, that is, from discrimination based on "SOGI." Kevin *really* doesn't want gays to get that wedding cake. Or access to the ER when their partner is dying, and other rights straight married couples take for granted.

3. Pornography will be outlawed.

Roberts hates porn more than he hates treason:

> Pornography...is not a political Gordian knot inextricably binding up disparate claims about free speech, property rights, sexual liberation, and child welfare. It has no claim to First Amendment protection. Its purveyors are child predators and misogynistic exploiters of women. Their product is as addictive as any illicit drug and as psychologically destructive as any crime. Pornography should be outlawed. The people who produce and distribute it should be imprisoned. Educators and public librarians who purvey it should be classed as registered sex offenders. And telecommunications and technology firms that facilitate its spread should be shuttered.

While it is certainly true that *some* adult online content is created by child predators and sex traffickers, not all of it is—not by a long shot. Why does Roberts, presumably a big believer in entrepreneurship, want to shutter an entire industry that generates $12-14 billion in domestic revenue annually? Did he have a bad experience on OnlyFans? Because, like, even *if* the U.S. were to criminalize adult content in the draconian way Roberts suggests, it's not like porn would stop being made or consumed. I guess he's cool with offshoring one of America's booming industries to China. Furthermore, why should sex workers be capriciously deprived of their right to free speech? As it is now, Neo-Nazis have an easier time publishing online their manifestos of hate than writers of erotica do their harmless smut.

And don't bring up the Bible. Jesus had just one notable female friend: Mary Magdalene. And we all know what she did for a living.

4. Trans individuals will be targeted for eradication.

Judge Potter Stewart famously said that he couldn't define porn, but he knew it when he saw it. Roberts has a very specific, and dangerously wrong, definition. The ellipsis in the previous quoted section is this dependent clause, in which Roberts elaborates on what *he* thinks porn is:

> Pornography, manifested today in the omnipresent propagation of transgender ideology and sexualization of children, for instance…

Putting aside for a moment the (unintended, I assume) implication that Roberts considers trans ideology and sexualized children erotic—for what is pornography if not commercialized erotic desire?—he is, by expressly connecting these things to pornography, suggesting that trans people are all sex objects, inherently X-rated, and therefore not suitable for public view. This is both untrue and harmful to that highly vulnerable population.

Literally the first recommendation in the Project 2025 book is that we "Restore the family as the centerpiece of American life and protect our children." Why does Roberts not want to protect trans children? Oh, right, he already told us: he prefers to believe that they don't exist.

But here's the reality: God may not exist. Jesus may not exist. But trans kids absolutely do.

5. **Blastocysts, zygotes, and embryos have more rights than women.**

If you're going to take away one paragraph from *Mandate for Leadership*, it's this one:

> Finally, conservatives should gratefully celebrate the greatest pro-family win in a generation: overturning *Roe v. Wade*, a decision that for five decades made a mockery of our Constitution and facilitated the deaths of tens of millions of unborn children. But the *Dobbs* decision is just the beginning. Conservatives in the states and in Washington, including in the next conservative Administration, should push as hard as possible to protect the unborn in every jurisdiction in America. In particular, the next conservative President should work with Congress to enact the most robust protections for the unborn that Congress will support while deploying existing federal powers to protect innocent life and vigorously complying with statutory bans on the federal funding of abortion.

Copy and paste it. Share it with your friends who "don't like politics" and think "Biden and Trump are both bad."

As discussed previously, the Cowboy Catholic and his Leonard Leo-backed extremists *want to ban abortion at the federal level.* They have stated this unequivocally, time and again. Trump is their vehicle for doing so. And once abortion is outlawed, they'll come for contraception, because these religious zealots harbor the erroneous belief that sex is for procreation only and not pleasure, and therefore semen denied access to the

Fallopian tubes by a latex sheath is no different than dilation and evacuation.

6. Women can and should die in childbirth.

This is, for my money, the most ominous sentence in the entire foreword:

> Conservatives should ardently pursue these pro-life and pro-family policies while recognizing the many women who find themselves in immensely difficult and often tragic situations and the heroism of every choice to become a mother.

Recognizing the many women who find themselves in immensely difficult and often tragic situations is not the same thing as *protecting the lives of* the many women who find themselves in immensely difficult and often tragic situations. It's clear the Roberts crew is going to eschew the latter to protect the unviable blastocysts they're pleased to call "the unborn." And what's this hokum about heroism? That sounds like a play on Horace: *Dulce et decorum est pro nondum nato mori.*[22] That's absolutely *terrifying*.

7. Forced-birth babies or babies born to dead mothers should be given to the state.

"Alternative options to abortion," Roberts writes, "especially adoption, should receive federal and state support." Given the fact that many, many more women will be dying in childbirth in a reign of Donald I, it's hard not to read this as encouragement for the MAGA

---

[22] It is sweet and proper to die for the Unborn.

state to collect these babies and send them to good Christian hetero homes.

8. The administrative state should be dismantled.

The idea of taking a wrecking ball to the federal government—to dismantle the institutions that safe-guard the air we breathe and the water we drink, that oversee our education system, that protect the LGBTQ community and other minority groups from discrim-ination, that keep our borders secure—is a Stephen K. Bannon hobbyhorse and also, as discussed, a major theme of that NRx Bible, the Unabomber Manifesto (see Chapter 6). Bannon and Ted Kaczynski are both 1) assholes, 2) criminals, 3) lunatics, and 4) nihilists. We should not listen to them!

If he had his druthers, Roberts would cripple, if not do away with entirely, the EPA, the Department of Education, the DOJ, the Pentagon, the State Department, and Homeland Security. At least, those are the agencies he singles out as being corrupt beyond measure.

> And despite its gaudy price tag, the federal budget is not even close to the worst example of this corruption. That distinction belongs to the "Administrative State," the dismantling of which must a top priority for the next conservative President. The term Administrative State refers to the policymaking work done by the bureaucracies of all the federal government's departments, agen-cies, and millions of employees.

Those millions of employees would be suddenly out of work. This is something Roberts has considered and dismissed with a shrug. To paraphrase the genocidal Papal legate Arnaud Amalric: Fire them all, let God sort them out. As he told the *New York Times*:

> People will lose their jobs. Hopefully their lives are able to flourish in spite of that. Buildings will be shut down. Hopefully they can be repurposed for private industry. But the administrative state — most importantly, what we're trying to destroy is the political influence it has over individual American sovereignty, and the only way to do that, or one of the ways to do that, is to diminish the number of unelected bureaucrats who are wielding that power instead of Congress.

They may also be coming for unemployment insurance; I haven't read that far into the rest of the book.

9. Wanting to ensure that the planet can sustain human life after 2050 is "extremism."

At this point, the only scientists who don't think global warming/climate change is real are sellouts and kooks funded by the fossil fuel industry. Climate protestors are gluing their hands to tarmacs and tennis courts. Kids are throwing soup at Van Goghs. It's a genuine crisis, and it's so big and scary that it's frankly impossible for me to fully wrap my head around it. If *I* lack the mental resources to process it, chances are, the family at the football game in Waco, Texas, is similarly hindered. Which doesn't make what's happening any less real or any less dangerous.

Roberts doesn't see it that way:

"Cheap grace" aptly describes the Left's love affair with environmental extremism. Those who suffer most from the policies environmentalism would have us enact are the aged, poor, and vulnerable. It is not a political cause, but a pseudo-religion meant to baptize liberals' ruthless pursuit of absolute power in the holy water of environmental virtue. At its very heart, environmental extremism is decidedly anti-human. Stewardship and conservation are supplanted by population control and economic regression. Environmental ideologues would ban the fuels that run almost all of the world's cars, planes, factories, farms, and electricity grids. Abandoning confidence in human resilience and creativity in responding to the challenges of the future would raise impediments to the most meaningful human activities. They would stand human affairs on their head, regarding human activity itself as fundamentally a threat to be sacrificed to the god of nature.

As Rone Tempest points out in his excellent Wyofile profile of Roberts, the Cowboy Catholic is fond of the expression "knows what time it is," which he uses as a compliment. So it's somewhat ironic that the climate clock is ticking, and Kevin has no idea how late the hour is.

10. Everyone should have the right to discriminate against anyone or anything because free speech!

Roberts shows his true colors here:

Ultimately, the Left does not believe that all men are created equal—they think *they* are special. They certainly don't think all people have an unalienable right to pursue the good life. They think only they themselves have such a right along with a moral responsibility to make decisions for everyone else. They don't think any citizen, state, business, church, or charity should be allowed any freedom until they first bend the knee.

What he's really saying is that the government has no right to impose civil rights protections on the people. That's what he means by "bend the knee." Christian schools should be allowed to be whites-only! Golf courses should be allowed to not allow membership to Jews! Bakeries and website designers should be allowed to not accept jobs from gays! How *dare* the federal government try to tell us God-fearing white Christians what to do!

PANDERING TO HIS AUDIENCE, Roberts begins his piece with a hagiographical ode to Ronald Reagan. But even this is misleading.

First of all, if Reagan, famous Cold Warrior, suddenly returned to life today, he would read the answer to the question of whether it is in the interest of the United States to help Ukraine beat Russia that Roberts gave the *New York Times*—

> Yes, *comma*, if we do so in a way that is responsible with the people's money, that articulates what the end game is, that is solely focused on military aid. And frankly, also recognizes that the United States of America, in both Democrat and Republican administrations, had a role in creating this conflict. Now, Putin and Russia deserve the blame. I've been very clear about that. Having said that, it was

our saber-rattling about Ukraine entering NATO that is one of the many factors that led to this. And so, yes, it's on the doorstep of a democratic Europe. We want the Ukrainians to win. But it would also be really helpful if the Germans, and the French in particular, would do more to support their neighbor.

—and find the nearest blunt object to (metaphorically) beat him over the head with. In that response, Roberts is parroting well-known Kremlin talking points and ceding the role of democracy's global guardian to *[reads quote again to make sure it's real]*...France? *France*!?! For shame!

More importantly: Roberts includes this quote from Reagan's First Inaugural Address as governor of California, delivered on January 5, 1967:

Freedom is a fragile thing and it's never more than one generation away from extinction. It is not ours by way of inheritance; it must be fought for and defended constantly by each generation[.]

What he doesn't provide is the context. In that part of the speech, Reagan was talking about the peaceful transition of power from one governor to the next—"the orderly transfer of administrative authority by direction of the people," as he put it that sunshiny day. "And this is the simple magic of the commonplace routine, which makes it a near miracle to many of the world's inhabitants: this continuing fact that the people, by democratic process, can delegate power, and yet retain the custody of it."

In other words, Roberts has quoted Reagan celebrating the peaceful transfer of power *in a book designed for an incoming administration of Donald Trump, an open insurrectionist*—the only president we've ever had who *refused* to heed that "simple magic" and vouchsafe "the orderly transfer of administrative authority." Is Roberts *intending* to be ironical here? Is he trolling us?

Here is the full quote, which Roberts abridges, perhaps because he doesn't want his readers contemplating the last line:

> Perhaps you and I have lived too long with this miracle to properly be appreciative. Freedom is a fragile thing, and it's never more than one generation away from extinction. It is not ours by way of inheritance; it must be fought for and defended constantly by each generation, for it comes only once to a people. And those in world history who have known freedom and then lost it have never known it again.

I have never agreed more with anything Ronald Reagan said.

We have managed to preserve our liberty for now, but if Trump wins—and the Cowboy Catholic and his cronies ram through the plans laid out in *Mandate for Leadership*—the grand American experiment won't see its 250th birthday.

Freedom is a fragile thing, and fragile things are easy to break.

VIII

REPUBLICANS IN NAME ONLY
This is not your grandfather's GOP

The Argument: The Party of Lincoln and the Party of Reagan is now the Party of Trump— the MAGA Party.

IN SEPTEMBER, Utah Senator Mitt Romney announced that he would not seek re-election when his term ends in January 2025. "I have spent my last 25 years in public service of one kind or another. At the end of another term, I'd be in my mid-eighties," he said. "Frankly, it's time for a new generation of leaders. They're the ones that need to make the decisions that will shape the world they will be living in."

After taking swipes at both POTUS and FPOTUS, he continued: "Political motivations too often impede the solutions that these challenges demand. The next generation of leaders must take America to the next stage of global leadership."

To step down and pass the torch before age and infirmity sets in is a noble impulse. That Romney has watched the public deterioration of Dianne Feinstein and Mitch McConnell probably informed this decision. But would he be quite so eager to hang up the spikes if the GOP—a party that nominated him for president not that long ago—had not gone off the rails? "It's pretty clear that the party is inclined to a populist demagogue message," he told the *Washington Post*, using two words where one—*fascist*—would have sufficed.

That's one way of saying it. Another is this: the Republican Party that Mitt Romney knew and loved and believed in no longer exists. That era is over. The Old Guard GOP are either dead, gone, or on the way out. The party of Nixon and Reagan, Bush and Cheney, Romney and McCain, Mitch McConnell and Lindsey Graham has become the party of Marjorie Taylor Greene, Jim Jordan, Matt Gaetz, and Donald Trump.

In the past, Republican popularity with voters derived from: 1) the GOP's traditionalist "family values" stance, 2) its commitment to law and order, 3) its reputation as being stronger on national security, and 4) its "fiscal conservative" economic agenda: cut taxes, rein in spending. Even in the boom times, the Republican plank was more hat than cattle. But now? None of those characterizations are even remotely accurate, if in fact they ever were. Let's take a look:

"Family Values"

I have often disagreed with Romney on matters large
and small, but he is, without question, a man of character and high moral standing. Today's Republican Party
offers no one with that kind of integrity. There is no
honor among thieves.

Also in September, Lauren Boebert, a rising star
within the new Republican Party, was thrown out of
a regional production of *Beetlejuice: The Musical* for…
causing a disturbance. As the *Denver Post* reported:

> The incident report states that after receiving the
> intermission warning, about five minutes into the
> second act security officials received "another com-
> plaint about the patrons being loud and at the
> time (they) were recording." Taking pictures or
> recording is not permitted at shows.

The report quotes one of the ushers: "They told me
they would not leave. I told them that they need to leave
the theater and if they do not, they will be trespassing.
The patrons said they would not leave. I told them I
would (be) going to get Denver Police. They said go
get them."

Subsequent video revealed that Boebert, who was
wearing a low-cut spaghetti-strap dress, was macking
down with her date—later revealed to be a Democrat
who owns a gay- and drag-friendly bar. "Macking down"
means that he was fondling her suddenly-more-ample
breasts, and she was grabbing at his crotch like she was
changing gears on her stick-shift. Footage also showed
her insouciantly vaping.

This matters because, first, there were plenty of kids
in attendance. Not that the presence of minors has

stopped Boebert's gentleman companions before: On January 28, 2004, when Lauren Roberts was 17 (the age of consent in Colorado) and Jayson Boebert was 23, Jayson was arrested at a bowling alley for showing his tattoo to some underage girls. He was arrested because the tattoo, apparently, is on his penis.

Second, Boebert has been outspoken in her condemnation of drag shows specifically and the LGBTQ community generally. Remember her idiotic tweet? "Take your children to Church," she advised, "not drag bars." She is a raging hypocrite who thinks the rules don't apply to her—or her disgusting family.

There are, of course, plenty of other examples of egregious GOP hypocrisy regarding family values. Boebert's gross display is only the most memorable.

Law and Order

Earlier this year, the Texas State Senate voted to acquit the state's impeached attorney general, Ken Paxton, on all charges, despite his obvious and glaring guilt. Paxton, who has also been under federal indictment for years now, is so breathtakingly corrupt that even members of his own party, including Dade Phelan, the Speaker of the Texas House of Representatives, pushed to impeach him.

In a statement after the acquittal, Phelan said, rightly, that Paxton "clearly abused his power, compromised his agency and its employees and moved mountains to protect and benefit himself. The Senate's refusal to remove Ken Paxton from office, is, however, not the end of this matter. Ken Paxton is the subject of multiple other lawsuit, indictments and investigations. If new facts continue to come out, those who allow him to keep his office will have much to answer for."

There is no rule of law in Texas.

But it gets worse. Mike Allen of Axios reports that the state senators were *pressured* to acquit the crooked AG, a big Donald Trump ally: "National Republicans organized an under-the-radar campaign of outside conservative pressure on the Texas senators designed to neutralize mainstream media coverage, top strategists tell me. This outside unofficial team operated independently of the Paxton legal operation—like 'a super PAC without the money,' a top GOP strategist said."

This is straight-up mob shit. This is Vito and Carmine showing up at your office, saying, "Helluva government job you got here. Be a shame if anything were to happen to it."

There are plenty of other examples of brazen Republican criminality—Trump *did* try to overthrow the government in a violent coup attempt, after all—but this is a biggie.

National Security

As he himself has admitted, and as we have all seen, Trump, the former president and the presumptive 2024 GOP nominee, kept boxes—many, many boxes—of classified documents in a bathroom at Mar-a-Lago, a private event space that is among the least secure facilities in the country. The documents in those boxes related to nuclear secrets, military information, and intelligence activity. You know, things that keep us safe. And he didn't even leave the boxes near the *gilded* toilet.

ABC News reported that Trump used some of the classified documents as scrap paper, to make to-do lists for his administrative assistant, Molly Michael. Worse, he appears to have instructed her to lie to federal agents about the provenance of the boxes of classified material: "Sources said that after Trump heard the FBI wanted to interview Michael last year, Trump allegedly told her, 'You don't know anything about the boxes.'"

The ABC News report then says, "It's unclear exactly what he meant by that," but anyone who has watched even half an episode of *The Sopranos* knows precisely what he meant by that.

This is the Republican nominee.

Fiscal Conservatism

Fiscal conservatives like Rand Paul are forever warning about the dangers of unsustainable national debt. They are so hyper-focused on this issue, it can almost be characterized as a kink. And yet Republican presidents routinely spend like Saudi royals buying former Trump officials—and the last two have been the worst culprits since the Civil War.

ProPublica released a study on the national debt in the last week of the Trump presidency. It paints a bleak picture:

> The national debt has risen by almost $7.8 trillion during Trump's time in office. That's nearly twice as much as what Americans owe on student loans, car loans, credit cards and every other type of debt other than mortgages, combined, according to data from the Federal Reserve Bank of New York. It amounts to about $23,500 in new federal debt for every person in the country.

The growth in the annual deficit under Trump ranks as the third-biggest increase, relative to the size of the economy, of any U.S. presidential administration, according to a calculation by a leading Washington budget maven, Eugene Steuerle, co-founder of the Urban-Brookings Tax Policy Center. And unlike George W. Bush and Abraham Lincoln, who oversaw the larger relative increases in deficits, Trump did not launch two foreign conflicts or have to pay for a civil war.

While the pandemic certainly contributed to Trump's unrestrained spending, it's not accurate to pin the blame on that exclusively. "The combination of Trump's 2017 tax cut and the lack of any serious spending restraint helped both the deficit and the debt soar," the *ProPublica* authors write. "So when the once-in-a-lifetime viral disaster slammed our country and we threw more than $3 trillion into COVID-19-related stimulus, there was no longer any margin for error."

This recklessness, plus the disastrous trillions George W. Bush wasted on tax cuts for the rich and his useless Middle East wars, will cripple our economy for generations. And yet Rand Paul and his ilk will merrily endorse the Republican candidate, who would, if elected, continue to rob the Treasury to enrich his cronies.

THE REPUBLICAN PARTY BRAND is strong. The myths and lies persist. Many if not most people respond more to "culture war" wedge issues and colorful personalities than, you know, reality. And while elephants have long memories, American voters do not.

"People respond to new news," Romney said in a *WaPo* interview. "They don't respond to old news. I mean, January 6th is old news. The documents, it's old news. The call to [Georgia Secretary of State Brad] Raffensperger, it's old news."The death of over a million Americans of covid-19 due to Trump's mismanagement of the pandemic response is also old news, so old that Romney forgot to mention it.

The old GOP is dead. The Republican Party has been appropriated by deviants, crooks, liars, and profligates. But come November, will anyone remember?

IX

THIRD PARTY POOPERS
Unsafe at any historical moment

*The Argument: A vote for a third party
candidate is a vote for Trump.*

In 2000, I was one of 2,882,955 Americans to vote
for Ralph Nader for president. I was young, idealistic,
and disillusioned with what I felt was a lack of progress by the national Democratic Party. I scoffed at the
primary system, which had somehow managed, in both
parties, to boot out the two exemplary candidates (Bill
Bradley and John McCain) and keep the two ho-hum
ones (Al Gore and George W. Bush). So I said "fuck
it" and pulled the lever—back then, there was still an
actual lever—for Ralph.

In my defense, I lived in solidly blue New York, and was thus afforded the luxury of casting what amounted to a meaningless protest vote. Were I registered in a swing state, I'd certainly have gone with Gore. (I have a friend who lived in Florida at the time and voted for—oh dear—John Hagelin, a sort of woo-woo precursor to Marianne Williamson. Let's just say she came to regret her decision.)

Also in my defense: I was dumb. I didn't fully understand the political system. In 1992, the first presidential election in which I was old enough to vote, I *wrote in* Al Gore, because I liked him better than Bill Clinton. Eight years later, I didn't vote for Tipper's hubby even though he was the Democratic candidate. See? Dumb.

With that said, I had what I believed were good reasons for going with Nader. In a piece I published on my now-defunct blog on October 17, 2000, I explained what the Green Party candidate was for:

- More regulation on large corporations. It's a subject for another column, but it's scary how few corporations own so many media outlets
- Affordable universal health care, based on the Canadian and Western European model
- Solving the public housing and public transportation problems ("The only public housing we're putting money into is the construction of more prisons.")
- Free public college education; improved public elementary and high schools
- Minimum wage increase ($5.15 an hour is not enough to get drunk in New York City, even during Happy Hour; Nader would double it)

- Investing in solar power, which would preserve the environment and eliminate our dependency on foreign oil in one fell swoop

Those are all solid reasons. And they were talked about, again and again, at a rally I attended at Madison Square Garden, where a slew of celebrities came on stage to sing the praises of Ralph Nader. "The night began with the MC, Phil Donahue, lambasting Bush and Gore for not addressing key issues," I wrote back then. "Then came the speakers and presenters, Susan Sarandon, Tim Robbins (in the guise of faux Republican Senator Bob Roberts), Ani di Franco, Ben Harper, Patti Smith, Jimmy Fallon, Bill Murray, and Eddie Vedder among them."

The last speaker before the candidate himself was Michael Moore. I've long since pegged the disheveled filmmaker as a self-important, self-aggrandizing, rabble-rousing provocateur—and perhaps a Republican in disguise—but at the time, I thought he was the proverbial cat's meow.

To a sold-out Garden, Moore presented his case. "If you don't vote your conscience now, when will you?" he pleaded. "Don't make a decision based on fear." He also said this: "I've heard people say, 'I'd vote for Nader, but I don't want to waste my vote.' Now I think we all agree that a Bush presidency would be hellaciously awful. But if you vote for the lesser of two evils, you're still voting for evil."

In the state of Florida, 97,488 people took his advice, voting for Nader instead of Gore. My friend was one of 2,281 to vote her conscience and go with Hagelin. Another 1,804 fearlessly opted for Monica Moorehead of the Workers World Party. A mere 562 Floridians abstained from deciding between two supposed evils, instead choosing Socialist Workers Party candidate James Harris.

Bush won Florida—and with it, the general election—by 537 votes.

Five. Hundred. Thirty. Seven.

IN AMERICAN POLITICS TODAY, it doesn't take courage to follow the party line. You don't need a backbone to hurl pot shots at the other side. To stir up hate and recrimination. To gum up the works. To refuse to cooperate. This moment demands American leaders and citizens alike declare their freedom from the anger and divisiveness that are ruining our politics and most importantly, our country. A United Front. We must recommit to the fundamental beliefs that have historically united Americans and provided a common understanding of who we are and where we hope to go.

Doesn't that sound lovely? It should. It's verbiage from the website of No Labels, a well-funded political concern which, as far as I can tell, was created to ratfuck the 2024 election. They have done their research and determined that Americans don't like all the squabbling in Washington. If people could only get along, and speak truth to power without fear, and focus on what unites us rather than what divides us, the country will finally be the *United* States of America! This is an idealistic vision that animates films like *Mr. Smith Goes to Washington* and TV programs like *The West Wing*. You know, works of fiction. It's something we can all get behind—but for the pesky fact that it ignores reality.

A third party candidate has never won a presidential election—has never come close. And because a two-party system is baked into the architecture of our government, a third party candidate will never win a presidential election (unless it supplants one of the two major-party slots, as the GOP did before the Civil War). So if you vote for a third party candidate, as I shall explain, you are in effect voting for the major-party candidate you like *less*.

Third party candidates make the same appeals today that Ralph Nader did in 2000, that Ross Perot did in 1992, that Teddy Roosevelt did in 1912: common sense, common ground, common good, common man. It *sounds* fantastic, but as Bernie Sanders can well attest, talking about doing something and actually getting it done are two wildly different things.

Let's debunk some particularly seductive third party talking points:

The lesser of two evils is still evil.

This is not the historical moment for an ethical purity test. In 2024, the Republican Party is running four-times-indicted, twice-impeached criminal con man, adjudicated rapist, and wannabe strongman Donald Trump. If you have the opportunity to vote against Nazis, vote against Nazis, because if they get into power, you won't be voting ever again.

Too much money is allocated for defense.

This was a big talking point in 2000, one I totally agreed with. "We have no known enemy; why are we wasting all these resources on military spending?" I know better now. For one thing, not all the money allocated to defense is used to buy weapons. A lot of useful technology comes out of the DoD: the internet, to name just one. For another, a lot of livelihoods of a lot of Americans is tied to that spending. And, most importantly, the *Pax Americana* exists because the United States is so unfathomably powerful. Many if not most of the military operations we've engaged in since 1945 were ill-advised if not flat-out malevolent; no argument there. But a strong U.S. military has created a relatively peaceful Western world for eight decades. That's a good thing. We want to keep that going.

Stop the military-industrial complex.

Conspiracy theorists love this one. Eisenhower famously warned against the burgeoning power of the "military-industrial complex" in his Farewell Address. Which, yes, for sure, be wary of that. But Biden *withdrew U.S. forces from Afghanistan*, guys. How was that not a giant "eff you" to the military-industrial complex, such as it is? And while he, as the leader of the free world, has leant his support to Ukraine, there has been no talk of committing U.S. troops to the cause. As president, Biden is more interested in domestic improvements—infrastructure, factories, unions, that kind of thing—than in making war.

Demand ceasefire in Ukraine now.

Putin invaded a sovereign nation. If the war stopped right now, even temporarily, Russia would keep all of the territory in Eastern Ukraine it has seized. We all want peace, but the way to achieve peace is not for the Ukrainians to surrender to a genocidal madman. And anyone saying otherwise—or blaming Biden for scuttling the end of the war, as RFK, Jr. has done—is disseminating Kremlin propaganda, knowingly or not.

There is no centrist candidate who represents most Americans.

Yes there is, people, and his name is Joseph Robinette Biden, Jr.! Reality check: The GOP as currently constituted is slightly to the right of Hammurabi. Since 1980, the entire political landscape has shifted in that direction. The rank-and-file Democrats *are* centrists. The party *really does* represent what a majority of Americans want. Alas, they are really, really bad at communicating this to voters. And the media sucks at reporting on it.

Progress isn't happening fast enough.

It's easy to *talk* about the progress that needs to happen. Any old grouch can stand on a soapbox and grouse about the minimum wage. Actually doing something about it is much, much harder—and generally, it takes the president working in lockstep with a House and Senate of the same political party. Bernie Sanders has been in Washington for over three decades. He talks a big game, but his track record of legislation is mortifyingly puny. As president, he would have little ability to get things done, because he isn't a member of the Democratic Party, and thus has no real sway over anyone in Congress. RFK, Jr. would be even worse. The surest way to achieve progress is to let Biden and Harris do what they've been doing, which is oversee the most progressive administration of my lifetime. The other side, meanwhile, is running a serial sexual assailant who brags about how he made *Dobbs* happen—in other words, how *he took a right away from us.*

The existing political system is moribund and corrupt.

Oh, it needs a facelift for sure, if not reconstructive surgery. The Electoral College is a patently anti-democratic vestige from the days of slavery. So is the system of allocation of senators. And we need a lot more Justices on the Supreme Court, to moot the malign influence of the Leonard Leo cabal. But real changes to the political structures can only happen when vociferous popular opinion meshes with a president and Congress of the same party, who can then enact legislation to implement those tweaks. The time to reform the system is not during a presidential election, and even if it were, the way to achieve reform is not by casting a protest vote.

The two parties are the same.

See Chapter 7. Republicans in red states have criminalized a woman's right to choose, while refusing to implement even the most anodyne gun regulations. Also, they are trying to eradicate the wall between church and state and eliminate trans people from public life. The GOP of 2024 is a party of active fascists. Democrats are not.

A THIRD PARTY CANDIDATE has never won the White House. A third party candidate will never win the White House. A third party candidate can only siphon votes away from the mainstream candidate whose politics are closer to those of the third party candidate.

Ross Perot, the most successful third party candidate of my lifetime, got 19,743,821 votes in 1992, a whopping 19 percent. Wanna guess how many electoral votes he got? I'll give you a hint: it's the number you can't divide by. The Bull Moose Party's Teddy Roosevelt banked the most electoral votes of any third party candidate: 88 of 531, back in 1912. That wasn't nearly enough to win the White House. And, like, he was *Teddy Roosevelt*, one of the five best presidents ever. His bust is on Mount Rushmore. But without the backing of one of the two major parties, TR could only muster a paltry 27 percent of the vote.

Sizing up the potential third party candidates for 2024, I detect no Teddy Roosevelts, only an uninspired gaggle of crackpots, chaos agents, and grifters. To run from the left in 2024, a candidate must answer the question, "Do you really think you can do better than Joe Biden, the best president we've had since Eisenhower?" with "Yes, obviously, of course!" Let's take a look at the field:

Robert F. Kennedy, Jr.

Say what you will about Ralph Nader, but as a legal activist, he was instrumental in the 1966 passage of the National Traffic and Motor Vehicle Safety Act, which has saved countless lives. Kennedy is best known for promoting vaccine disinformation and debunked junk science, which does the opposite. If you went back in time to the 1880s and explained to parents of young children who just died from diphtheria that that horrific disease would be eradicated, safely and forever, by a simple jab, and then offered it to them and their remaining children, how many of those grief-stricken moms and dads do you think would refuse it? Vaccines are a miracle of modern medicine. RFK, Jr. is too dumb to see through the most obvious of Russian ops—the vaccine disinformation—which means he is hopeless against the more sophisticated ones.

Cornel West

West is a charismatic guy, but I seem to recall him going on *Bill Maher* in 2016 and telling the audience that there was no fundamental difference between Hillary Clinton and Donald Trump, and therefore everyone should vote for "Sister" Jill Stein. You know, Jill Stein: Putin's dinner guest. A vote for Jill Stein was a vote for Trump in 2016, and a vote for Cornel West is a vote for Trump in 2024. West is way too smart not to be aware of this.

Marianne Williamson

She was Oprah's spiritual advisor. What could go wrong?

It's easy to make fun of these people, and we should mock them to oblivion. But the third party threat to Biden is no laughing matter. As the investigative journalist Dave Troy and others have pointed out, the fascist playbook is to create a "red-brown alliance" of the far left and the far right, with the ultimate aim of undermining democracy.

The lesser of two evils is still evil, true. But what Michael Moore failed to disclose in 2000 is that supporting a third party candidate on the left is, in effect, a vote for the *greater* of two evils.

Concerned about Biden's age? Dude, Trump is only four years younger and in way worse physical shape.

Not a fan of Kamala Harris? Ask yourself the question: Is it *Kamala* you're not a fan of, or the idea of having a Black woman in the White House?

Don't like that Biden is selling arms to Israel? Neither do I. But here's what Trump will do, if he's in power: let Bibi Netanyahu remove every last Palestinian from

Gaza, either by displacing them or killing them outright; raze it; pave it; and let Bibi's family friend Jared Kushner build luxury condos on the coastline to sell to Russian oligarchs. The way to help the people of Gaza is to keep putting pressure on the Biden Administration, but *not* to deny Joe the vote. Under Trump, there will be *more* violence in Gaza, but no legal way to protest in his dictatorship.

A vote for RFK, Jr. is a vote for Trump.

A vote for Cornel West is a vote for Trump.

A write-in vote for a non-candidate who passes your ethical purity test is a vote for Trump.

An empty ballot is a vote for Trump.

Not voting is voting for Trump.

Like it or not, the only way—the *only* way—to vote *against* Trump is to vote *for* Joe Biden. It's Biden or bust. Literally.

X

AMERICAN STRONGMAN, REVISITED
A summary of the life of Donald Trump

The Argument: This beast should not be president again.

THIS IS THE REAL Donald John Trump.

The father was loaded, parlaying a little bit of capital—and a long association with the Genovese crime family—into a Queens real estate empire. The son was a difficult child. He got bad grades and was often in trouble at school. Once he punched a teacher in the mouth. Unable to control him, his parents shipped him off to military school. The experience seemed only to hone his bullying skills. It was a serial killer's childhood.

Nevertheless, he was his father's favorite. If he got into trouble, he could always rely on his old man to bail him out. During Vietnam, his dad arranged for a podiatrist—a tenant in one of his properties—to concoct a medical excuse (bone spurs) so he could avoid military service. He did poorly on his SATs but still managed to get into an Ivy League school—admission was easier back then, especially if you had money. His academic career was so lackluster that he *still* won't allow anyone to see his grades, 50 years after the fact.

After graduating, he went into the family real estate business. But he wasn't satisfied with Queens. He wanted to make it in Manhattan. He wanted real fame, real fortune. This required working with the Gambino crime family, which controlled New York's premier borough. As always, his old man helped make it happen for him.

The KGB began cultivating him in the early 1980s. He was an easy mark: vain, stupid, amoral, sex-crazed, and desperate for cash. By the middle of that decade he was using condos in the tower that bore his family's name to launder money for Russian organized crime figures. He liked doing business with crooks. They paid in cash, and if things went sideways, they would never sue.

He married a beauty from the Eastern Bloc, a smart, ebullient immigrant whose parents were hardline Communists, allegedly in league with Czechoslovakian intelligence. They had three children, two boys and a girl. When he got bored—and when her success began to overshadow his—he divorced her to marry his side piece, an actress. They had a daughter together. When he got bored, he left his second wife and eventually married his third, like the first an Eastern European stunner with hardliner parents. They had a son.

During the entire length of these three marriages, he had numerous affairs. He cavorted with models and beauty queens. He bought the Miss Universe franchise and used it as a vehicle to sexually harass and assault the contestants. When his oldest daughter was a teenager, he had her sign with a modeling agency whose owner was notorious for sexual assault. He seemed to have a thing for the daughter, and once remarked that if they were not related, they would be dating. He palled around with a New York financier who was always surrounded by very young women—girls, as it turned out. (That financier would be convicted of procuring a child for prostitution, and, much later, for much more.) He was accused of sexual assault by dozens of women. He raped a well-known journalist in the dressing room of a department store.

His business ventures almost always failed. Many of his companies went bankrupt. He opened a casino and it went bust. He inherited hundreds of millions of dollars from his father, and he squandered it. He lied to magazines about his fortune. He called reporters posing as a PR guy for himself. He almost singlehandedly ruined a rival pro football league. He announced gifts to charities and then didn't give over the money.

Banks refused to do business with him, because he routinely did not make good on his commitments. He stiffed contractors. He hired illegal immigrants to work for him and paid them slave wages. His only profitable enterprise was laundering money for his Russian clients. The building that bears his name became a hub of Russian organized crime activity in the United States.

Then came the TV show. It was the brainchild of a reality show producer whose original idea was to make a program featuring Vladimir Putin. He was portrayed as a rich, successful, self-made businessman. None of those things were true, but viewers believed the myth, the legend. He was good at playing the part. He enjoyed uttering his catchphrase: *You're fired*. The executive at the TV station who had greenlighted the show moved from that network to the top cable news network in the United States, overseeing the entire news operation.

Despite having never held elected office—his only real political experience consisted of calling for the execution of the Central Park Five and disseminating the lie that the country's first Black president was born in Kenya—he decided to run for president. Media outlets, especially the cable news network run by the friend who had greenlighted his TV show, covered him as if he were actually the character he played on the show—as if none of the horrible things he'd done in the past had ever happened. The correspondent covering his campaign for the country's paper of record was more concerned with maintaining access than investigating the truth of his chequered past—a truth that could be found in her own newspaper's archives.

He began his campaign with racist statements. He appropriated a slogan from the 1930s, when the American Nazi Party was popular in New York. He was overtly sexist, overtly racist, overtly in league with the leader of our nation's longtime adversary. He mocked a disabled journalist at a rally. But the milquetoast Republican field could not stop him. None of them had been a character on a reality TV show, after all. He won the primary easily.

He railed against his Democratic political opponent. He knew people didn't trust her. He tried to tap into that lack of trust. He said she should be locked up. He accused her of unspecific crimes. He kept invoking her emails. In one of the debates, she said that all 17 U.S. intelligence agencies agreed that Russia had hacked the DNC emails. She called him "Putin's puppet." He seethed and stalked her on the stage. He looked more like Jack the Ripper than a serious political candidate.

He lost the election by 2.8 million votes. But an uncanny series of events combined with the ham-handed Electoral College thwarted her victory. Because of Russia, because of the FBI Director, because of Facebook micro-targeting, because of the racism and sexism that permeates American politics, he won.

He appointed unqualified cronies and family members to key positions. His daughter and his son-in-law were his closest advisors. The Secretary of State was a retired oil executive who gutted the department. The Secretary of Education wanted to destroy the Department of Education. The Attorney General was a racist. The National Security Advisor was a traitor. And so on.

He spent approximately one third of his 1461 days in office visiting one of his properties, including a whopping 298 days on a golf course he owned. Taxpayers paid the tab on every single one of those visits—hotel rooms for him, his family, Secret Service, and all the members of his entourage. The final tab was something like $100 million over four years, a significant portion of which went right into his pocket, because he owned the properties where all those people stayed and dined. Being president was a profitable job for him—one of the most profitable he's ever had.

He obstructed justice many times, in obvious ways. He fired the FBI Director because he didn't want his ties to Russia investigated. He sent goons to the offices of his doctor, and they made off with his medical records. He paid a porn star hush money. He extorted the president of an ally, threatening to withhold arms unless that president investigated his political rival. He hosted Russian leaders in the Oval Office, laughing as he offered them classified information. On the national stage, he capitulated to Putin time and again. He tried to intimidate the Georgia Secretary of State into fudging the election results.

He was twice impeached. His apologists in the Senate let him off both times. He pardoned his many criminal accomplices, including three former campaign advisors and the traitor national security advisor.

In the early days of the pandemic, he insisted the coronavirus would just disappear. He blamed China. He blamed Democratic governors in blue states. He and his son-in-law intentionally sabotaged the pandemic response because they thought it would help him win re-election if people in New York and California died. Many millions of dollars of Paycheck Protection Program (*PPP*) loans went unaccounted for. He railed against masks. He railed against vaccines. He politicized the pandemic. This all resulted in hundreds of thousands of American deaths—more than died in the Civil War. When he got covid, he tried to pretend that it was no big deal, even as his blood oxygen dipped to dangerous levels. He was given special medical treatment unavailable to most people.

Months before election day, he claimed the election would be stolen. He believed mail-in votes would hurt him, so he installed a lummox at the postal service, who set about destroying sorting machines. He spent months conniving about ways to stay in power despite what he knew would be a humiliating defeat at the ballot box.

He lost by seven million votes. He refused to concede. He said the votes were rigged. He said the election was stolen. He tried everything he could think of to game the system. On January 6, the day the votes from state electors were being certified, he encouraged the crowd in

Washington to besiege the Capitol. He attempted a coup. To stay in power, he was willing to let his loyal VP die.

He tried to overthrow the government

He's still trying to do that.

For this monster—this bully and brat; this racist and rapist; this mob money launderer and tax cheat; this thrice-married philanderer; this sadistic strongman who allowed a plague to take hold because he thought all that death would help him; this sore loser who attacked our democracy and did everything in his power to overturn the election; this dismal, disgraceful, deplorable failure of a human being—a quarter of the country, and maybe more, are willing to do almost anything, including kill and be killed.

What can the rest of us do about it? What I wrote at the end of *Dirty Rubles* remains true six years later: "We can vote, for one thing, for candidates who will work to oppose Trump. We can lend our energies to those campaigns. We can continue to call our Senators and Representatives in Congress and voice our concerns. We can protest. We can march. We can also—and this is important—tell the truth, loudly and unapologetically. If the American people understand the extent of Trump's crimes, his greed, his cruelty, his contempt for the country, its citizens, its traditions, its laws…if the truth, the whole truth, and nothing but the truth can be *reliably* told…then Trump will fall, and fall hard."

The real Donald Trump is a Rough Beast.

The United States is slouching towards dictatorship.

But if we vote accordingly—and only if we vote accordingly—we shall prevail.

—*GMO*
New Paltz, NY
May 8, 2024

ACKNOWLEDGEMENTS

First: Stephanie Koff, my friend, *Five 8* cohost, and fellow traveler in what may well be a simulation, has helped me maintain my sanity for the last five years. She also taught me everything I know about Trump's dalliances with mobsters and spies. This book would not have been possible without her. In addition to making me guffaw every week, the brilliantly funny Donnie Gillespie, aka Chunk, made some wonderful cover art. Big thanks to Kim Pardi, Jackie Roemer, and Pam Murtaugh for reading and proofing early drafts.

I'm grateful to everyone at MSW Media—Allison Gill, Kanai Willians, Molly Hawkey, Kimberley Johnson—for their help with my podcast. I've learned so much from the guests who have been gracious enough to come on the show, and I thank them, too, especially Tom Carter, Victor Rud, Brynn Tannehill, Ruth Ben-Ghiat, Lisa Graves, Alex Aronson, Noel Casler, Moscow Never Sleeps, Jen Mercieca, Kurt Andersen,

Rachel Slade, Vince Scafaria, Aaron Harris, Lou Neu, Jen Taub, Arthur Snell, Sandi Bachom, Ethan Bearman, Shireen Mitchell, Amanda Moore, Jack Bryan, Steven Beschloss, Cliff Schecter, Dahlia Lithwick, Manisha Sinha, and the indefatigable Gal Suburban.

I am so grateful for, and to, all of my PREVAIL subscribers. Thanks for reading and sharing my work, and for making the comments section such a pleasure. Thanks to the *Five 8* community for making Friday nights such a joy—in particular Marie Cast, Jen Griffin, Sharon Dymond, Arthur Klassen, Kindness, Cheryl Fillekes, Stephen Koff, Barbara and Jeff Black, and Dexter Haven, whose keen intellect and keener insight I appreciate so much.

I've been highly critical of the mainstream media these last six years, and rightly so, but I want to acknowledge the many excellent journalists whose crack investigative reporting is essential to understanding the MAGA universe: Katherine Eban, Craig Unger, Luke Harding, Heidi Przybyla, Suzanne Craig, Rone Tempest, the *ProPublica* crew, Katherine Stewart, Nina Burleigh, Will Bunch, Jay Michaelson, and Hugo Lowell, to name a few.

Big thanks to Liz Pickett, William Crane, Michelle Girard, Robbie Harris, Owen Robinson, Aja Raden, Nia Molinari, Joanie Vee, Claudia Black, Heidi Cuda, Ronlyn Domingue, Cheri Jacobus, Diana Spechler, Beth Ward, Tally Briggs, Rosanna Arquette, and the intrepid and inspiring Zarina Zabrisky. Shout out to Stacy Lew, Stuart Syvret, Jim Stewartson, Ivo Gatzinski, Crow Woman, Kathy, EOB727, Leslie Rosenberger, Dawn O'Leary, Natasha Trash, Mimi Fischer, GG By the Sea, Rosalyn Lander, Paulina, Donna McKee, Tom Bolin, Julie Scarrone, Cinnawhee, Geronimo de los Cielos, Foggy Ozark, Jereen Swan, Kate Bennett, Vati Ammatri, William Becker, Lolo, JRance, Katie O'Grady,

Jonathan Simon, Lorraine Evanoff, Leslie Polsen & Brian Keeler, Bob Manojlovich, Martha Acuña, Ravi Chandran, Cameron Baillie, Grant Delaney, Kirsten Smith, Gail (Chicago), Cal Lash, Susan Linehan, Earl Heflinger, Helen Stajninger, Lynell, Mary Pat Sercu, Jeri Chilcutt, Patrick Daniels, James Cioe, Amy Starks, Judy Luchsinger, Karen Bennett, Ryan Byrne, Cathy Swanson, Steve B, Dawn Westlake, Michelle Kantor, Jenny Cohn, Whitney McKnight, Elisabeth Grace, Helen Cowan, Mary Giles, Wendy Jacobson, Bill Serle, Sandy Lewis, Mark Plotkin, Liz Selleck, K.M. Koger, Lynne Corbett, Angel Levine, Lisbeth Farnum, John Melendez, Paul Zolbrod, and Monique Ponsot.

Finally, gratitude and much love to my family: my mom, Janice; Franklin St. John and the rest of the St. John clan; my lovely, talented, and extremely patient wife, Stephanie; and our two kids, Dominick and Milo, both of whom will be voting in a presidential election for the first time this November and would really, really, *really* like me to STFU about Trump.

NOTES & SOURCES

PREFACE

Covid death figure:
Logan Lutton, Medical Economics, "Coronavirus case numbers in the United States: January 20, 2021."
https://www.medicaleconomics.com/view/coronavirus-case-numbers-in-the-united-states-january-20-2021-update

Economy:
Dominic Rushe, The Guardian, "US economy shrank by 3.5% in 2020, the worst year since second world war," January 28, 2021.
https://www.theguardian.com/business/2021/jan/28/us-economy-shrank-2020-worst-year-since-second-world-war

Debt:
David Manuel, "US National Debt Soars By Nearly $8 Trillion Under President Trump" January 16, 2021.
https://www.davemanuel.com/2021/01/16/president-trump-national-debt/

Crappy job approval:
Jeffrey M. Jones, Gallup, "Last Trump Job Approval 34%; Average Is Record-Low 41%," January 21, 2021.
https://news.gallup.com/poll/328637/last-trump-job-approval-average-record-low.aspx

Protests:
Per Wikipedia, the five biggest are the George Floyd Protests, Earth Day, the 2017 Women's March, March for Our Lives and the 2018 Women's March. Only Earth Day did not happen when Trump was in office.

Emoluments:
Dan Alexander, Forbes, "Trump's Businesses Hauled in $2.4 Billion During he Four Years He Served as President," July 19, 2021.
https://www.forbes.com/sites/danalexander/2021/07/19/trumps-business-hauled-in-24-billion-during-four-years-he-served-as-president/?sh=1a33e16210c0

Eric Trump Cancer Charity:
Dan Alexander, Forbes, "How Donald Trump Shifted Kids-Cancer Charity Money Into His Business," June 6, 2017.
https://www.forbes.com/sites/danalexander/2017/06/06/how-donald-trump-shifted-kids-cancer-charity-money-into-his-business/?sh=1bd803176b4a

CHAPTER 1: LIES

Inflated net worth:
Jonathan Greenberg, Washington Post, "Trump Lied to Me About His Wealth to Get Onto the Forbes 400," April 20, 2018.
https://www.washingtonpost.com/outlook/trump-lied-to-me-about-his-wealth-to-get-onto-the-forbes-400-here-are-the-tapes/2018/04/20/ac762b08-4287-11e8-8569-26fda6b404c7_story.html

Walter Reed:
Libby Cathey, ABC News, "Trump makes unannounced visit to Walter Reed Medical Center for 'quick exam and labs,' says White House," November 17, 2019.

https://abcnews.go.com/US/trump-makes-unannounced-visit-walter-reed-medical-center/story?id=67082769

Drugs
Greg Olear, PREVAIL, "Full Disclosure: An Interview with Noel Casler," May 1, 2020.
https://gregolear.substack.com/p/full-disclosure-an-interview-with

Ibid, "Comfortably Dumb: Drugs in the Trump White House," February 13, 2024.
https://gregolear.substack.com/p/comfortably-dumb-drugs-in-the-trump

Egypt
Katelyn Polantz, Evan Perez and Jeremy Herb, CNN, "Exclusive: Feds chased suspected foreign link to Trump's 2016 campaign cash for three years," October 14, 2020.
https://www.cnn.com/2020/10/14/politics/trump-campaign-donation-investigation/index.html

Caputo
Sharon LaFraniere, NYT, "Trump Health Aide Pushes Bizarre Conspiracies and Warns of Armed Revolt," September 14, 2020.
https://www.nytimes.com/2020/09/14/us/politics/caputo-virus.html

HIV in Indiana
GREGG GONSALVES and FORREST CRAWFORD, Politico, "How Mike Pence Made Indiana's HIV Outbreak Worse," March 2, 2020.
https://www.politico.com/news/magazine/2020/03/02/how-mike-pence-made-indianas-hiv-outbreak-worse-118648

Jared Kushner & the Pandemic
See Chapter 4

Bezmenov's warning
https://www.youtube.com/watch?v=IQPsKvG6WMI&t=84s

CHAPTER 2: ORGANIZED CRIME & FOREIGN INFLUENCE

General:
Stephanie Koff, "The World Beneath," podcast, 2021.
https://open.spotify.com/show/4WUWWHUlpXar1MnmwocmQu?si=fc1e312890644fac

Lincoln's Bible (Koff) and Louise Neu, Citjourno, "Poke the Bear," November 3, 2017.
http://www.citjourno.org/page-1

Luke Harding, *Collusion: Secret Meetings, Dirty Money, and How Russia Helped Donald Trump Win*, 2017.

Craig Unger, *American Kompromat: How the KGB Cultivated Donald Trump, and Related Tales of Sex, Greed, Power, and Treachery*, 2022.

Craig Unger, House of Trump, House of Putin, 2018.

Robert I, Friedman, Red Mafiya: How the Russian Mob Has Invaded America, 2000.

Wayne Barrett, Trump: The Deals and the Downfall, 1992.

Yuri Shvets media interview:
Narativ Live, "Russia on the Brink 2," February 10, 2022.
https://www.youtube.com/watch?v=yzb1dNxiwfQ

Crime as an economy:
Reuters, "Crime one of the world's "top 20 economies": U.N." 2012.
https://www.theglobaleconomy.com/rankings/gdp_share/

Condos:
Craig Unger, The New Republic, "Trump's Russian Laundromat," July 13, 2017.
https://newrepublic.com/article/143586/trumps-russian-laundromat-trump-tower-luxury-high-rises-dirty-money-international-crime-syndicate

Ibid, Washington Post, "Trump's businesses are full of dirty Russian money. The scandal is that it's legal," March 29, 2019. https://www.washingtonpost.com/outlook/trumps-businesses-are-full-of-dirty-russian-money-the-scandal-is-thats-legal/2019/03/29/11b812da-5171-11e9-88a1-ed346f0ec94f_story.html

Trump meets Russians:
Paula Spahn, Washington Post, "When Trump hoped to meet Gorbachev in Manhattan," December 3, 1988. https://www.washingtonpost.com/lifestyle/style/from-the-archives-when-trump-hoped-to-meet-gorbachev-in-manhattan/2017/07/10/3f570b42-658c-11e7-a1d7-9a32c91c6f40_story.html

Trump in New Hampshire:
Michael Cruse, Politico Magazine, "The True Story of Donald Trump's First Campaign Speech—in 1987," February 2016. https://www.politico.com/magazine/story/2016/02/donald-trump-first-campaign-speech-new-hampshire-1987-213595/

Trump tax loss:
David Usborne, The Independent, "Donald Trump's leaked 1995 tax return shows loss so enormous 'he could have avoided paying taxes for years," October 2, 2016. https://www.independent.co.uk/news/world/americas/us-politics/donald-trump-tax-return-1995-losses-avoid-paying-leak-times-a7341196.html

Atlantic City overvalue:
The Australian, "Donald Trump: The Deals and the Mafia Dons."

State of New Jersey Gaming Report, which highlights Trump's underworld ties: https://a.fastcompany.net/asset_files/-/2016/03/04/Trump 1992MOB.pdf

Sammy Gravano, "Our Thing," Season 4, Episode 3, "Donald Trump," February 18, 2022.

https://www.audible.com/es_US/podcast/Our-Thing-Season-4-Episode-3-Donald-Trump-Sammy-The-Bull-Gravano/B09STPJQP8

Interview with Craig Unger:
PREVAIL podcast, "House of Unger, House of Olear," October 15, 2021.
https://gregolear.substack.com/p/the-blind-eye-of-the-fbi-with-craig

Interview with James Kallstrom:
NPR, Morning Edition, "Comey Faces Sharp Criticism; Ex-FBI Official Calls Clinton A 'Criminal'," November 1, 2016.
https://www.npr.org/2016/11/01/500183744/comey-faces-sharp-criticism-ex-fbi-official-calls-clinton-a-criminal

Andy McCabe, statement, March 17, 2018.
https://www.cnn.com/2018/03/16/politics/mccabe-fired-statement-fbi-deputy-director/index.html

James Comey, *Higher Loyalty*, 2018.

CHAPTER 3: CORRUPT PARDONS

Mueller Report

Senate Volume 5
SELECT COMMITTEE ON INTELLIGENCE, UNITED STATES SENATE, ON RUSSIAN ACTIVE MEASURES CAMPAIGNS AND INTERFERENCE IN THE 2016 U.S. ELECTION, VOLUME 5: COUNTERINTELLIGENCE THREATS AND VULNERABILITIES, Augus 18, 2020.
https://www.intelligence.senate.gov/sites/default/files/documents/report_volume5.pdf

Barton's House report:
JUSTICE UNDONE: CLEMENCY DECISIONS IN THE CLINTON WHITE HOUSE, SECOND REPORT by the COMMITTEE ON GOVERNMENT REFORM Volume 1 of 3, May 14, 2001.

https://www.congress.gov/congressional-report/107th-congress/house-report/454/1

Marc Rich pardon:
Eric N. Berg, NYT, "MARC RICH INDICTED IN VAST TAX EVASION CASE," September 20, 1983.
https://www.nytimes.com/1983/09/20/business/marc-rich-indicted-in-vast-tax-evasion-case.html

Tranche released:
Josh Gerstein, Politico, "Clinton camp questions FBI release of Marc Rich pardon files," November 1, 2016.
https://www.politico.com/story/2016/11/marc-rich-pardon-files-230590

Ken Kurson Court Complaint, October 22, 2020.
https://www.documentcloud.org/documents/20459996-ken-kurson-court-complaint

Johan E. Bromwich, NYT, "Ken Kurson, Kushner Ally Pardoned by Trump, Takes Plea Deal," February 16, 2022.
https://www.nytimes.com/2022/02/16/nyregion/ken-kurson-trump-kushner-plea.html

Ken Kurson Misdemeanors
Bess Levin, Vanity Fair, "The Best People: Kushner Pal Pardoned by Trump Pleads Guilty to Cyberstalking," February 2022.
https://www.vanityfair.com/news/2022/02/ken-kurson-donald-trump-cyberstalking

AP, "Former N.Y.C. top cop Bernard Kerik gets four years in federal prison," February 18, 2010.
https://www.nj.com/news/2010/02/former_nyc_top_cop_bernard_ker.html

January 6 Committee Index:
https://www.cnn.com/2022/06/12/politics/january-6-committee-jared-kushner/index.html

Noelle Dunphy's lawsuit against Rudy Giuliani, May 15, 2023:
https://iapps.courts.state.ny.us/nyscef/ViewDocument?doc
Index=ayMPHcCh5eCKqo1g4gB42A==

Trump wishes Ghislaine Maxwell well:
https://www.youtube.com/watch?v=jC2jsRrzCrs

Reps. Request pardons:
Scott Wong, NBC News, "Jan. 6 panel reveals GOP lawmakers
sought Trump pardons after Capitol attack," June 23, 2022.
https://www.nbcnews.com/politics/congress/jan-6-panel-
names-republican-lawmakers-sought-pardons-trump-rcna35090

Broidy
DOJ press release, "Elliott Broidy Pleads Guilty for Back-Channel
Lobbying Campaign to Drop 1MDB Investigation and Remove
a Chinese Foreign National," October 20, 2020.
https://www.justice.gov/opa/pr/elliott-broidy-pleads-guilty-
back-channel-lobbying-campaign-drop-1mdb-investigation-and

Erickson
DOJ press release, "Sioux Falls Man Sentenced for Wire Fraud
and Money Laundering," July 6, 2020.
https://www.justice.gov/usao-sd/pr/sioux-falls-man-
sentenced-wire-fraud-and-money-laundering-1

Angela Kennecke, Keloland, "Trump pardon called Paul Erickson
bilking $1.2 million from investors a 'minor financial crime,'"
January 20, 2021.
https://www.keloland.com/news/investigates/trump-pardon-
called-paul-erickson-bilking-1-2-million-from-investors-a-minor-
financial-crime/

Jesse Benton
DOJ press release, "Political Consultant Sentenced for Scheme
Involving Illegal Foreign Campaign Contribution to 2016
Presidential Campaign," February 17, 2023.
https://www.justice.gov/opa/pr/political-consultant-sentenced-
scheme-involving-illegal-foreign-campaign-contribution-2016#:~:-

text=In%20November%202022%2C%20Benton%20was,be%20
filed%20with%20the%20FEC.

Russ Choma, Mother Jones, "GOP Operative Sentenced to 18
Months for Funneling Russian Money to Trump Campaign,"
February 17, 2023.
https://www.motherjones.com/politics/2023/02/jesse-benton-
donald-trump/

Ed Henry
Kim Chandler, AP, "Former Alabama lawmaker Ed Henry pardoned
by Trump," January 20, 2021.
https://apnews.com/article/donald-trump-alabama-montgomery-
ed-henry-medicare-5d3a4cbf2664eb3662f9dc1c6ad98041

Dinesh D'Souza
FBI press release, "Dinesh D'Souza Sentenced in Manhattan
Federal Court to Five Years of Probation for Campaign Finance
Fraud," September 23, 2014.
https://www.fbi.gov/contact-us/field-offices/newyork/news/
press-releases/dinesh-dsouza-sentenced-in-manhattan-federa
l-court-to-five-years-of-probation-for-campaign-finance-
fraud#:~:text=Preet%20Bharara%2C%20the%20United%20
States,pled%20guilty%20to%20violating%20the

Helly Nahmad
Sarah Bahr, NYT, "Trump Pardons Hillel Nahmad, Madison
Avenue Art Dealer," January 20, 2021.
https://www.nytimes.com/2021/01/20/arts/design/
trump-pardons-helly-nahmad.html

CHAPTER 4: COVID, JAN 6

Messonnier
CDC Telebriefing transcript:
https://archive.cdc.gov/#/details?url=https://www.cdc.gov/media/
releases/2020/t0225-cdc-telebriefing-covid-19.html

Will Feuer, CNBC, "Watch: US health officials hold news briefing on coronavirus outbreak," February 25, 2020.
https://www.cnbc.com/2020/02/25/watch-us-health-officials-hold-news-briefing-on-coronavirus-outbreak.html

Birx appointment
Press release, "Vice President Pence Announces Ambassador Debbie Birx to Serve as the White House Coronavirus Response Coordinator," February 27, 2020.
https://trumpwhitehouse.archives.gov/briefings-statements/vice-president-pence-announces-ambassador-debbie-birx-serve-white-house-coronavirus-response-coordinator/

Sunnier forecast
Ian Schwartz, Real Clear Politics, "Dr. Birx: Coronavirus Data Doesn't Match The Doomsday Media Predictions," March 26, 2020.
https://www.realclearpolitics.com/video/2020/03/26/dr_birx_coronavirus_data_doesnt_match_the_doomsday_media_predictions_or_analysis.html

Trump knew covid was serious and lied about it:
Bob Woodward, *Rage*, September 15, 2020.

Erik Hayden, The Atlantic, "Bush's 9/11 Classroom Reaction Was Meant to Project 'Calm'," July 29, 2011.
https://www.theatlantic.com/politics/archive/2011/07/bushs-911-classroom-reaction-was-meant-project-calm/353430/

Katherine Eban, Vanity Fair, "How Jared Kushner's Secret Testing Plan Went 'Poof Into Thin Air,'" July 30, 2020.
https://www.vanityfair.com/news/2020/07/how-jared-kushners-secret-testing-plan-went-poof-into-thin-air

"This is flu"
White House Briefing Statements, February 27, 2020.
https://www.whitehouse.gov/briefings-statements/remarks-president-trump-vice-president-pence-members-coronavirus-task-force-press-conference/

Covid deaths
"April Deadly Month," Washington Post, April 2020.
https://www.washingtonpost.com/graphics/2020/national/
coronavirus-april-deadly-month/

Trump has covid
His tweet, October 2, 2020.

Trump sicker than reported
Noah Weiland, Maggie Haberman, Mark Mazzetti and Annie
Karni, NYT, "Trump Was Sicker Than Acknowledged With
Covid-19," February 11, 2021.
https://www.nytimes.com/2021/02/11/us/politics/trump-
coronavirus.html

Noah Higgins-Dunn, CNBC, "U.S. reports second-highest daily
number of Covid cases on Election Day as scientists warn of a
dangerous winter," November 6, 2020.
https://www.cnbc.com/2020/11/04/us-reports-second-
highest-daily-number-of-covid-cases-on-election-day-as-
scientists-warn-of-a-dangerous-winter.html

Kusher blocks transfer
Joshua Zitser, Business Insider, "Jared Kushner blocked Biden's
access to COVID-19 planning in the final days of the Trump era,
former aide says," December 20, 2020.
https://www.businessinsider.com/jared-kushner-refused-
biden-access-covid-19-planning-former-aide-2022-12

Failed US policies led to more covid deaths
Richard Parker, University of Connecticut Law School, "Why
America's Response to the Covid-19 Pandemic Failed: Lessons
From New Zealand's Success," February 9, 2021.
https://digitalcommons.lib.uconn.edu/law_papers/528/

Birx's bad numbers
Ian Schwartz, Real Clear Politics, "Dr. Birx: Coronavirus Data
Doesn't Match The Doomsday Media Predictions," March 26, 2020.

https://www.realclearpolitics.com/video/2020/03/26/dr_birx_coronavirus_data_doesnt_match_the_doomsday_media_predictions_or_analysis.html

RIP Diamond
Ken Meyer, Mediaite, "Trump Eulogizes Diamond By Saying He Hardly Knew Silk, Ranting About the 2020 Election, and Complaining About the Length of the Funeral," January 22, 2023. https://www.mediaite.com/trump/trump-eulogizes-diamond-by-saying-he-hardly-knew-silk-ranting-about-the-2020-election-and-complaining-about-the-length-of-the-funeral/

Pence's son convinces him to not overthrow government
Martin Pengelly, The Guardian, "Pence's son reportedly convinced him to stand up to Trump over January 6," November 29, 2023. https://www.theguardian.com/us-news/2023/nov/29/mike-pence-son-trump-jan-6#:~:text=%E2%80%9CDad%2C%20you%20took%20the%20same,January%206%20attack%20on%20Congress.

Sedition
Greg Olear, DAME Magazine, "This is What Sedition Looks Like," January 11, 2021. https://www.damemagazine.com/2021/01/11/this-is-what-sedition-looks-like/

Impeachment fear
Jake Lahut, Business Insider, "Congressman says some GOP lawmakers are 'paralyzed with fear,' and think their families will be attacked if they vote for impeachment," January 13, 2021. https://www.businessinsider.com/threats-against-republican-congress-jason-crow-impeachment-vote-paralyzed-fear-2021-1

Complicit Congressmen
Teo Armus, Washington Post, "A 'Stop the Steal' organizer, now banned by Twitter, said three GOP lawmakers helped plan his D.C. rally," January 13, 2021. https://www.washingtonpost.com/nation/2021/01/13/ali-alexander-capitol-biggs-gosar/

Recon tour
Nicholas Katzban, North Jersey, "Rep. Mikie Sherrill says Congress members gave 'reconnaissance' tours day before Capitol raid," January 12, 2021.
https://www.northjersey.com/story/news/politics/2021/01/12/mikie-sherrill-pro-trump-rioters-got-tour-congress-members/6648386002/

Cawthorn packing heat
Sebastian Murdock, Huffington Post, "GOP Rep. Madison Cawthorn Was Armed With Gun During Insurrection He Helped Incite," January 13, 2021.
https://www.huffpost.com/entry/gop-rep-madison-cawthorn-said-he-was-armed-with-gun-during-capitol-insurrection_n_5fff2597c5b691806c4ea2bc

Liz Cheney statement
January 12, 2021
https://www.politico.com/news/2021/01/12/liz-cheney-trump-impeachment-statement-458394

CHAPTER 5: DICTATORSHIP

Trump dictatorship
Robert Kagan, Washington Post, "A Trump dictatorship is increasingly inevitable. We should stop pretending," November 30, 2023.
https://www.washingtonpost.com/opinions/2023/11/30/trump-dictator-2024-election-robert-kagan/

Godwin's Law
Mike Godwin, Washington Post, "Yes, it's okay to compare Trump to Hitler. Don't let me stop you," December 20, 2023.
https://www.washingtonpost.com/opinions/2023/12/20/godwins-law-trump-hitler-comparisons/

Trump cultivating Hitler
Jennifer Mercieca, Resolute Square, "Trump is Running for Dictator," December 7, 2023.

https://resolutesquare.com/articles/6YwCV82rAuGjXkvi0lkFkn/
trump-is-running-for-dictator

Ibid, *Demagogue for President*, 2020.

Brynn Tannehill, *American Fascism* (2021).

Kash Patel on War Room
https://www.mediamatters.org/steve-bannon/steve-bannon-and
-kash-patel-tout-trumps-second-term-retribution-plan-just-not-
rhetoric

CHAPTER 6: DARK ENLIGHTENMENT

Ted Kaczynski, *Industrial Society and Its Future* (1995).
https://www.washingtonpost.com/wp-srv/national/longterm/
unabomber/manifesto.text.htm

James Pogue, Vanity Fair, "Inside the New Right, Where Peter
Thiel Is Placing His Biggest Bets," April 2022.
https://www.vanityfair.com/news/2022/04/inside-the-new-right-
where-peter-thiel-is-placing-his-biggest-bets

IM1776, Yarvin interview
https://im1776.com/2021/09/03/curtis-yarvin-interview/

Curtis Yarvin, Gray Mirror, "A brief explanation of the cathedral,"
January 21, 2021
https://graymirror.substack.com/p/a-brief-explanation-of-the-
cathedral

Jason Wilson, The Guardian, "'Red Caesarism' is rightwing code
– and some Republicans are listening," October 1, 2023.
https://www.theguardian.com/world/2023/oct/01/red-caesar-
authoritarianism-republicans-extreme-right

RAGE
Erich Wagner, Government Execuive, "Trump Has Endorsed a Plan
to Purge the Civil Service of 'Rogue Bureaucrats'," July 27, 2022.

https://www.govexec.com/workforce/2022/07/trump-endorsed-plan-purge-civil-service-rogue-bureaucrats/375028/

Will Bunch, Philadelphia Inquirer, October 5, 2023. https://www.inquirer.com/opinion/red-caesar-right-american-dictatorship-20231005.html

Leo as woke
Michelle Goldberg, NYT, "The Right's Obsession With Wokeness Is a Sign of Weakness," March 10, 2023. https://www.nytimes.com/2023/03/10/opinion/republican-woke-focus.html?unlocked_article_code=KfHyhv16hOm1_Ny0Bahvp vQxIjA9u45o C1NaG68EZ4tnZw_A6Mwb2l Xtss-YY1JtPd4 ASaG9WGUzx BEm5Ow4jA69QEUbYKq69dq5-w3USPivt MOlzXVnyxZslM5ngskTF2bAypw5CHQYcCTsBcoDi hcER95K-eg3cix_8WCnTmsbPSAjMXAXdiMt1WO mzHTNF6ktGOfOo15IszOh9LQ2ZtibGCMvMBfW4MFUG QF3v5-9YEnz2tLo3EJ8rw_Z5jVVvWgqTrFqUc3H3 mlD416D5LeiQVhjMkeFgcQvtzd00Fh2NZygft65JO0a7 TVLMTNmetBlFuskof98fvayuc0&smid=url-share

Bannon as Leninist
Ronald Radosh, Daily Beast, "Steve Bannon, Trump's Top Guy, Told Me He Was 'a Leninist'," April 13, 2017. https://www.thedailybeast.com/steve-bannon-trumps-top-guy-told-me-he-was-a-leninist

Philip Rucker and Robert Costa, Washington Post, "Bannon vows a daily fight for 'deconstruction of the administrative state'," February 23, 2017. https://www.washingtonpost.com/politics/top-wh-strategist-vows-a-daily-fight-for-deconstruction-of-the-administrative-state/ 2017/02/23/03f6b8da-f9ea-11e6-bf01-d47f8cf9b643_story.html

Purge civil service
Eric Katz, Government Executive, "If Trump Is Reelected, His Aides Are Planning to Purge the Civil Service," July 22, 2022 https://www.govexec.com/workforce/2022/07/trump-reelected-aides-plan-purge-civil-service/374842/

CHAPTER 7: PROJECT 2025

Leonard Leo
Jeffrey Toobin, The New Yorker, "The Conservative Pipeline to the Supreme Court," April 17, 2017.
https://www.newyorker.com/magazine/2017/04/17/the-conservative-pipeline-to-the-supreme-court

Ed Whelan, The National Review, "Mistaken Attack by Andy Schlafly on Leonard Leo," December 9, 2016.
https://www.nationalreview.com/bench-memos/schlafly-attack-leonard-leo/

Jay Michaelson, Daily Beast, "The Secrets of Leonard Leo, the Man Behind Trump's Supreme Court Pick," Jul7 9, 2018.
https://www.thedailybeast.com/the-secrets-of-leonard-leo-the-man-behind-trumps-supreme-court-pick

Grace/Operation Paperclip
Jewish Telegraphic Agency, "Special to JTA Yeshiva U. Says It Cancelled Dinner Honoring U.S. Businessman Who Aided Convicted War," June 2, 1981.
https://www.jta.org/archive/special-to-jta-yeshiva-u-says-it-cancelled-dinner-honoring-u-s-businessman-who-aided-convicted-war

Heidi Przybyla, Politico, "Dark money and special deals: How Leonard Leo and his friends benefited from his judicial activism," March 1, 2023.
https://www.politico.com/news/2023/03/01/dark-money-leonard-leo-judicial-activism-00084864

Washington Post, "Judicial activist directed fees to Clarence Thomas's wife, urged 'no mention of Ginni'," May 4, 2023.
https://www.washingtonpost.com/investigations/2023/05/04/leonard-leo-clarence-ginni-thomas-conway/

Robert O'Harrow, Jr. and Shawn Boburg, Washington Post Investigations, May 21, 2019.

https://www.washingtonpost.com/graphics/2019/investigations/leonard-leo-federalists-society-courts/

Anne Nelson, The Washington Spectator, "How the CNP, a Republican Powerhouse, Helped Spawn Trumpism, Disrupted the Transfer of Power, and Stoked the Assault on the Capitol," February 22, 2021.
https://washingtonspectator.org/nelson-cnp/

Leo buys house in Maine:
https://sell-my-housee.blogspot.com/2019/08/why-did-trumps-judge-whisperer-buy.html

Barre Seid donation:
Andrew Perez, The Lever, and Andy Kroll and Justin Elliott, ProPublica, "How a Secretive Billionaire Handed His Fortune to the Architect of the Right-Wing Takeover of the Courts," August 22, 2022.

Nina Burleigh, New Republic, "Who Is Leonard Leo's Mysterious Dark Money King?" May 16, 2023.
https://newrepublic.com/article/172480/barre-seid-leonard-leo-dark-money-king

Kevin Roberts:
Jack Healy, NYT, "To Keep Free of Federal Reins, Wyoming Catholic College Rejects Student Aid," April 11, 2015.
https://www.nytimes.com/2015/04/12/us/to-keep-free-of-federal-reins-wyoming-catholic-college-rejects-student-aid.html

Rone Tempest, Wyofile, "Wyoming's 'Cowboy Catholic' could remake government if Trump wins," February 8, 2024.
https://wyofile.com/wyomings-catholic-cowboy-could-remake-government-if-trump-wins/

Lulu Garcia-Navarro, NYT Magazine, "Inside the Heritage Foundation's Plans for 'Institutionalizing Trumpism'," January 21, 2024.
https://www.nytimes.com/2024/01/21/magazine/heritage-foundation-kevin-roberts.html

Kevin Roberts, foreword to *Mandate for Leadership: The Conservative Promise* (2024)

Cleta Mitchell
Kyle Ingram, The News & Observer, "Challengers of NC law want court to force former Trump lawyer to comply with subpoena," January 31, 2024.
https://www.newsobserver.com/news/politics-government/article284929742.html#storylink=cpy

Porn industry revenue:
GITNUX MARKETDATA REPORT 2024
https://gitnux.org/pornography-industry-statistics/

Ronald Reagan's First Inaugural Address as Governor of CA
https://www.reaganlibrary.gov/archives/speech/january-5-1967-inaugural-address-public-ceremony

CHAPTER 8: GOP

Romney announcement:
https://www.romney.senate.gov/romney-releases-message-to-utahns-on-senate-reelection-plans/

Boebert at Beetlejuice:
John Aguilar, Denver Post, "Lauren Boebert escorted out of "Beetlejuice" musical in Denver after "causing a disturbance," September 12, 2023.
https://www.denverpost.com/2023/09/12/lauren-boebert-removed-beetlejuice-musical-denver/

Boebert video:
https://www.youtube.com/watch?v=UMgTuc2wl6U

Boebert boyfriend:
Joe Tacopino, New York Post, "Lauren Boebert breaks up with Democratic bar owner who groped her during 'Beetlejuice' date," September 18, 2023.

https://nypost.com/2023/09/18/lauren-boebert-breaks-up-with-man-who-groped-her-during-beetlejuice-date/

Jason Boebert arrest:
Anne Landman Blog.
https://annelandmanblog.com/wp-content/uploads/2020/10/Boebert-Jason-record-2.pdf

Zachary Petrizzo, Salon, "Lauren Boebert's husband did jail time for "lewd exposure" in a bowling alley. She was there," August 31, 2021.
https://www.salon.com/2021/08/31/lauren-boeberts-husband-did-jail-time-for-lewd-exposure-in-a-bowling-alley-she-was-there/

Boebert hypocrisy
Julia Reinsten, BuzzFeed, "Here's How Rep. Lauren Boebert Smeared LGBTQ People On Social Media Before Offering Prayers For The Victims Of The Colorado Springs Gay Club Shooting," November 21, 2022.
https://www.buzzfeednews.com/article/juliareinstein/lauren-boebert-twitter-lgbtq-colorado

Boebert son
Chris Perez, Westword, "Lauren Boebert's Son Allowed to Appear in Court Virtually Despite Bench Warrant for Prior No-Show," May 1, 2023.
https://www.westword.com/news/lauren-boebert-son-virtual-court-appearance-bench-warrant-no-show-16747454

Ken Paxton acquittal
Zach Despart, Texas Tribune, "Texas Attorney General Ken Paxton acquitted on all 16 articles of impeachment," September 16, 2023.
https://www.texastribune.org/2023/09/16/ken-paxton-acquitted-impeachment-texas-attorney-general/

Dade Phelan statement:
https://twitter.com/DadePhelan/status/1703123084566294981

Pressured to acquit Paxton:
Mike Allen, Axios, "How GOP Pressured Texas," September 17, 2023.
https://www.axios.com/newsletters/axios-am-hard-truths-806aa3bd-b7d0-425e-8815-89ded8fab51b.html?chunk=0& utm_campaign=axios_app#story0

Trump uses classified docs as scrap paper
Katherine Faulders, Mike Levine and Alexander Mallin, ABC News, "Trump wrote to-do lists for assistant on White House documents marked classified: Sources," September 18, 2023.
https://abcnews.go.com/US/trump-wrote-lists-assistant-white-house-documents-marked/story?id=103226113

Trump debt study
Allan Sloan and Cezary Podkul, Pro Publica, "Donald Trump Built a National Debt So Big (Even Before the Pandemic) That It'll Weigh Down the Economy for Years," January 14, 2021.
https://www.propublica.org/article/national-debt-trump

Romney not seeking reelection
Dan Balz, Washington Post, "Mitt Romney says he will not seek a second term in the Senate," September 13, 2023.
https://www.washingtonpost.com/politics/2023/09/13/mitt-romney-senate-reelection/

CHAPTER 9: THIRD PARTIES

RFK blames Biden
https://twitter.com/RobertKennedyJr/status/1670889423007805455

Anti vax is Russian deza
Julian Barnes, NYT, "Russian Disinformation Targets Vaccines and the Biden Administration," August 5, 2021.
https://www.nytimes.com/2021/08/05/us/politics/covid-vaccines-russian-disinformation.html

Horseshoe
Dave Troy: https://twitter.com/davetroy/status/16702232926
09724416

CHAPTER 10: REVIEW

Trump's inheritance
DAVID BARSTOW, SUSANNE CRAIG and RUSS
BUETTNER, NYT, "Trump Engaged in Suspect Tax Schemes
as He Reaped Riches From His Father," October 2, 2018.
https://www.nytimes.com/interactive/2018/10/02/us/politics/
donald-trump-tax-schemes-fred-trump.html

Maggie Haberman
Louise Neu & Lincoln's Bible, Citjourno, "Maggie Duranty,"
January 1, 2018.
http://www.citjourno.org/maggie1

Golf:
https://trumpgolfcount.com/

PPP Loans Unaccounted For
Aaron Gregg, Washington Post, "Trump administration won't
say who got $511 billion in taxpayer-backed coronavirus loans,"
June 11, 2020.
https://www.washingtonpost.com/business/2020/06/11/trump-
administration-wont-say-who-got-511-billion-taxpayer-
backed-coronavirus-loans/

Printed in Great Britain
by Amazon

42199682R00106